The Beloved of the Creator

The Beloved of the Creator

The Odyssey of
Catechist Mark Bassey Obotama

By
Raphael Mark Obotama

authorHOUSE®

AuthorHouse™
1663 Liberty Drive
Bloomington, IN 47403
www.authorhouse.com
Phone: 1-800-839-8640

Published by AuthorHouse   06/12/2013

ISBN: 978-1-4817-5130-8 (sc)
ISBN: 978-1-4817-5129-2 (e)

Library of Congress Control Number: 2013908342

DEDICATION

To the Memory of Catechist Mark Bassey Obotama.

and

The Medical Missionaries of Mary Sisters.

(without whom the biography of our Father
would have been shorter than this.)

Contents

Foreword

I am glad to have a copy of the book **The Beloved of the Creator** written by Rev. Fr. Raphael Obotama in memory of his late father, Catechist Mark Bassey Obotama (1926-2002) who slept in the Lord in 2002 at the age of seventy six years. As the family celebrates the tenth anniversary of the glorious exit of their illustrious father, this book has the nature of both biography and a primary source of information on the life and times of Catechist Obotama.

It is pertinent to note that Catechist Obotama's childhood as an orphan was not without set backs and difficult challenges. He was converted to Catholicism during his primary school days. With the assistance given to him by the Irish St. Patrick's Fathers and the Medical Missionaries of Mary Sisters, Catechist Obotama was able to start a trade and marry a good wife. The fruits of his works can be seen in the solid family upbringing and training of his God-fearing children who are serving in different areas in the Catholic Apostolate. Among the children are two Diocesan Priests and a daughter who is a nun and member of the MMM Congregation.

Catechist Obotama was well known to me. He was one of the pioneer Catechists who selflessly served the local Church in Ikot Ekpene Diocese since its creation in 1963. The memory of this great teacher cannot easily be forgotten by those who had the privilege of living and working with him. Personally I recall that, when my present home Parish, St. Joseph, Okon was under Urua Akpan Parish in the sixties, Catechist Obotama played a prominent role in the preparation of candidates, including myself, for Baptism and First Holy Communion.

He belonged to the first generation of Catechists who formed the Diocesan Catechists Association. He was a promoter of Marian Apostolate and League of the

Sacred Heart of Jesus by means of which he was able to establish Legion of Mary and the Sacred Heart centres in Ikot Ekpene Diocese. He was a man of prayer, deep spirituality and solid faith. He had great devotion and belief in the Eucharist. As he did when he was on earth, his life testimony, admonishes all ordained ministers and the entire lay faithful to believe in the Eucharist **for the whole life of the Church depends on that.** According to Rev. Fr. Raphael, his father Catechist Mark Obotama, **as a lay person, could tell by the way a priest celebrated Mass if the priest believed in the Sacrifice of the Mass and the Eucharist or not.** This is where the life of Catechist Obotama, poses a great challenge to our Catholic life and faith.

This Book, *The Beloved of the Creator* by Rev. Fr. Raphael Obotama, who also is the first son of Catechist Obotama is therefore a very befitting memorial for a man who lived a life worthy of emulation. There is no doubt that the impact of Catechist Obotama's life and teaching is still being felt today in Ikot Ekpene Diocese and beyond where those taught by him along with his children are serving the Church in different places and in various capacities. The simple style adopted in the writing of this book makes it easy to read.

+ Most Rev. Camillus A. Etokudoh
Bishop of Port Harcourt Catholic Diocese.

Catechist Mark Bassey Obotama
1926-2002

Testimonies

". . . Your father, as you know, was very dear to me too. He was a good Catholic man and a faithful Catechist."

—Most Rev. Ephraim S. Obot
—Former Bishop of Idah Catholic Diocese. (now deceased)

(Excerpt from a condolence message to the author, July 24, 2002)

"Your father did the right thing in giving you out to serve the Lord . . . may God give him a place with the saints in heaven."

—Most Rev. Joseph E. Ekuwem
Bishop of Uyo Catholic Diocese

(Excerpt from a condolence Message to the author, July 24, 2002)

Catechist Obotama was a good friend of mine. He was a good and dedicated catechist even after his retirement, a man of faith and a committed Christian. I was his last pastor on earth and I administered the last sacrament to him before he passed on to eternity on that Sunday morning. Surrounded by his children, he was conscious and responded to all the prayers said during the anointing. He received the Holy Eucharist joyfully and with that I knew he was prepared to leave the world. While the prayers and songs were going on he closed his eyes in acquiescence to the will of God. He died a good man and his death was really a celebration of life. I have no doubts that he has a place with God and the saints in heaven.

Rev. Monsignor James F. Iyire
Vicar General, Catholic Diocese of Ikot Ekpene.

1

And the Sun Rises

Wednesday, November 3, 1926 started in a very normal and unobtrusive manner in the little farming village of Ikot Inyang Udo in Essien Udim Local Government Area of Akwa Ibom State, Nigeria. Of course, there were no particular expectations for something out of the ordinary to occur, as the people were used to a routine life.

The village early morning chores mostly for women and children, had started as soon as the cocks began to crow, and one could hear the voices of the children who were running to and from the stream. Wine tappers and their assistants were trooping to their different plants to service the morning drips of fresh wine from the palm trees. The sun began its slow movement, rising elegantly from the east side of the village, casting golden light upon a village that depended on its illumination for most of their quotidian activities.

Thus, the village was going about its typical activities until the shrill cry of a baby emanated from a little hut behind the house of Obot Akpan Nna in Nto Akpan Nna family of Nto Udo Ikpa kindred, announcing the safe arrival of a baby boy delivered by his wife, Adiaha Udo Nnwa. That first cry signified that the baby was quite alive and bubbling. The event evoked hollers of jubilation from the traditional birth attendant and a few women who assisted at the delivery. She, the traditional birth attendant chanted a special tune, which signified the birth of a male child. This chant also attracted the womenfolk around the neighborhood, who trooped to see the new person who had come to join the household of Obot Akpan Nna.

As the neighbors arrived, a spontaneous singing and dancing erupted among the women while the men started yodeling. Within the traditional ethos of Annang nation, a child belongs to the whole village. The birth of one child is therefore a thing of joy for the whole community. The logic here is that Obot Akpan Nna had increased the family membership of Nto Akpan Nna and Nto Udo Ikpa kindred by yet another male member. This is no small feat, bringing a new male into a family. The Annangs celebrate life with pageantry, and this was a cause for celebration.

For Adiaha Udo Nnwa, like any other happy mother of a male child, she could now be certain of a secured place in the family especially as the mother of the first male child, Eka Akpan, for her husband Obot Akpan Nna.

That singular moment of this particular child's birth changed the mood of the village and, by extension, its history. Accordingly, the hitherto unknown village of Ikot Inyang Udo found its way into many national and international documents because of the birth of this little baby. The baby boy, who was later named Bassey by his proud father, lived to become Catechist Mark Bassey Obotama, a man of faith, a father and grandfather, blessed with many children and grandchildren.

When he was born, many members of his family did not profess the Christian or Catholic faith; therefore, he was not born into a Christian or Catholic family. At the event of his birth, all the traditional rituals that follow the birth of a child were in place. The Annangs were very religious before the arrival of Christianity, and they believed in life after death as the Christians do. But unlike Christians, they also believed in reincarnation. In most cases, the belief was that a child who came into a family must be a departed ancestor and, therefore, ceremonies and rituals to welcome him or her back were necessary. Other rituals were ones of purification and security. A very interesting aspect of this belief in life after death and even life before birth has a bearing in the Christian theology. Traditional rituals that formally accept the newborn into the family of the living were a *sine qua non* and as such, this newborn would not in any way be an exception. Of course, at the time of his birth no one knew he was going to be a catechist preaching against pagan rituals; they were caught up in the fact that this newborn baby was the first male child—*Akpan*. Therefore, there was no holding back on the required traditional rituals. The first child in Annang has a lot of responsibilities; therefore, he has to be prepared through rituals and grooming. He has to be very rich in cultural capital as a potential head of the family. Papa (the author's father) did not tell us about this other aspect of his early life, but looking at it through the lens of scholarship, there was no reason why his parents would not do as tradition demanded at that time. This had been (and in some cases still is) the general practice in traditional Africa. John Mbiti confirms the following: ". . . rituals are performed to give protection to the child as it begins a long journey in life . . ."[1]

As to why Papa did not tell us about these early life events, I can proffer two guesses: one, I think he did not want to scandalize us, because he had always wanted us to be truly Christian children. Second, he probably just wanted to bury his past in the sands of history, because he had embraced a new life and raised a new family. He did not actually believe in those old rituals now that he knew and served a true God.

---

[1]   Mbiti, J. S., Introduction to African Religion, Heinemann, 1991, p.90

For Obot Akpan Nna, the happiest day of his life was when he heard the cry of his first male child and held him in his hands—the dream of every Annang man. He could now be counted among those who have male children, and for any orthodox Annang man that is the zenith of success. Any casual person entering the compound that day could not fail to know who the father was without being told. Obot went into the barn and brought out the best yams he had preserved. Then he personally ran around the village to purchase condiments for the preparation of a very special pepper soup known locally as *mmong efere eka uman*—a spicy broth specially made on occasions like this, sometimes as stimulants for the baby's mother. Bottles of locally brewed gin called *akai kai* and pots of palm wine were available as neighbors began to pour in to celebrate the new baby. This little baby, who spent most of the day sleeping, was no doubt the object of attraction.

His mother was being attended to by the traditional birth attendant and some elderly women of the family. In-laws from Ekpenyong immediately arrived to celebrate their grandson, and the excited Obot spent the whole day entertaining guests and thanking his ancestors, who protected his wife through a safe delivery. The traditional birth attendant who assisted at the labor was lavishly rewarded before she went home while the neighbors continued their drinking spree.

Throughout the day, there was much drinking by the menfolk in the compound as they sat around telling stories and occasionally bursting into songs. The birth of a new child is always a cause for celebration, especially if it is a male child. Children are the future hope of the family. In this particular case, it was not just that he was a male child; it was very special because he was the *first* male child of Obot Akpan Nna. He therefore became the hope for the family's lineage to continue, and Obot had carved his family name in stone with the birth of an heir.

When the appropriate time came, the naming ceremony was conducted in the presence of the elders of the family, and the happy father named him Bassey. I must admit to a failure here on my part—I should have asked him why he was named Bassey given that this name is very particular of the Efiks, an ethnic group in the Calabar area, the southern part of the country. However, he grew with that name until his encounter with Christianity and his subsequent baptism later in life, when he took a new name and began his journey into Catholicism. This book is in your hands now because of a journey that was completely unplanned and unforeseen by humanity.

2

The Eclipse

*God's jewels are often sent to us in rough
packages . . .*

B. Simpson

In this earthly life, every living person arrives with
a *tabula-rasa*, or blank slate. It is only the Creator
who sees what is on the slate, because He is the author
of our future. We begin to write on the slate as soon
as we arrive on the earth, and our history is made up
of what is written on it. For some, life begins on a

smooth ground and rolls onto a rough surface, while some start on a rough ground and roll onto a smooth surface. Some stay on one side or the other all through life. As you read on, you will discover where Bassey fits in, in these categories.

Bassey's birth and early infancy were like any other child's in the traditional Annang society. He was blessed with good parents who lived up to their responsibilities and took care of him as demanded by the culture of their time. At that phase of life, Bassey's day was comprised of getting up late in the morning, eating breakfast prepared by a loving and caring mother, and running around chasing butterflies until he was called in at midday to come eat lunch. In the afternoon, he would be led by the hand to the village stream just a short walking distance away from their compound for a thorough bath, then back for dinner and to bed. That was a typical day for him, and in his juvenile mind, if that was all life took, then life was worth living. He was looking forward to a wonderful life in the future, with lots of opportunity accorded him by his birth order. Supported by loving parents, he imagined how he would live to be one of the richest people in the village. But that hope was shattered early in his childhood.

Tragedy visited him at an age when he was too young to process the reality unfolding before him. Quite unlike many children of his age, it did not take him long to discover that the life he was imagining before him was just a mirage. It slowly occurred to him that life had different faces and can change at any time without any warning. In most cases, life presents different faces to different people, but all of them share one uncanny characteristic: change.

Life's greatest attribute is its changing nature, sometimes for good, at other times for bad. This particular attribute caught the attention of an ancient philosopher Heraclitus, when he theorized some centuries ago that everything is in the state of change. He was merely stating the obvious. Life itself is a changeable and changing phenomenon; in life's journey change is inevitable. Every human being has to pass through this. It is part of human experience. I always say that life is an institution and we learn as we live, but such harsh lessons came rather too early and too swiftly into little Bassey's life. For him, everything about life was just what he experienced as a toddler. Like any other child, he had no reason to preempt what life would present to him in a not too distant future.

A thick dark cloud fell over the bright sunshine in little Bassey's life when the cold hands of death snatched his parents from him when he was just six years old, too young even to understand what death was. That was the tragedy that turned history around for him and set the course that would shape his future. Life was no longer the same and it set him on a journey comparable to that of our great father in faith: Abraham. No wonder a great deal of Bassey's life was propelled by fate rather than human assistance. This early circumstance in his life turned him into a man who put his faith in God rather than trusting in man. He looked up to God as his only hope. His life echoed the words of the psalmist, "For father and mother have left me: but the Lord had taken care of me" (Psalm 27:10). The Father of the orphan literally became Bassey's father as the events in his life gradually unfolded. Here the words of God through the mouth of the prophet Isaiah play out clearly, "I will be your God throughout your lifetime. I made you and I care for you" (Isaiah. 36: 4). God indeed kept His words with Bassey to the end, a God Bassey did not know through his parents but through his encounter with the Christian faith.

For several weeks after the death of his mother at the age of 5 he did not know what it was all about. He was still thinking that his mother had probably traveled and would return. Before he was able to come to terms with the reality of his mother's death, his father also died. His world in which he had barely spent 6 years now became, quite literally, an empty space.

Bassey was blessed to have a step-brother who took care of him briefly, but unfortunately, the step-brother also died. At this point, Bassey's eyes were opened to the hard facts of this wicked world. The straight road of his life which seemed promising at first had taken a U-turn. The hard reality of life was now staring at him. There was an eclipse in his life.

The early breakfast once prepared by his mother was not forthcoming, and sometimes he was not even sure of where his next meal would come from. He knew that he had to do something about the situation. He had to take care of himself if he was to survive the world around him that was changing before his eyes. He learned to take the bull by the horns at an age when other children were still being taken care of by their parents. He started taking care of himself, becoming both father and mother.

Bassey was barely 6 years old when he started taking care of himself. He had to endure the inconvenience of waking up very early in the morning to join some adults trekking from his village to Ikot Ekpene, a distance of about 30 kilometers, to sell *mfang oko*—some special multi-functional leaves used in wraping some food items by traders. Bassey had to run the whole distance in order to keep pace with the adults. Throughout these trips he could not join in their conversations because of his young age; he just trotted along quietly. Bassey then used the proceeds from his sales to take care of himself.

This unusual circumstance of his early childhood made him something of an introvert. He was just himself within his little world. Whatever was in his young mind during those moments, only God knew. Bassey built a virtual wall around himself, only opening up to a few people. This influenced his worldview and that of most members of his family even to this day.

3

~❧~

Stepping into Western education

One of the endearing hallmarks of the early missionary priests' ministries was the establishment of schools to give the local folks a western education. To encourage local people to see things from the missionaries' perspective, it was necessary to educate them. The missionaries calculated that establishing schools would also be a sure way of getting into the hinterlands and bringing the people closer to them, thereby encouraging them to embrace the Christian religion. The idea was that the school children would serve as links to their pagan parents. In fact, the Christian religion reached most of the local people through their children as they were converted in the schools. The schools did more than just teach the Christian religion, however; they laid a very successful foundation for the western culture. Almost every successful person in our part of the world today owes his or her success to this education brought by the missionaries. In light of this, one can count the work of the early missionaries as a huge success. A lot of children were drawn to this program. Mission schools were everywhere and they trained a number of local children who trooped there every morning for classes.

His early traumatic experience notwithstanding, Bassey was strongly attracted to this western education. It was not so popular among his people at that time because they clung to certain urban legends. His urge to be educated, however, overpowered the myth and the fear of the cost of education. At that time, he did not consider how he would be able to take care of the basic necessities that this education would demand of an orphan like he. As far as he was concerned, where there was a will there was always a way, and this personal philosophy came through in the end for him.

His journey into the realm of western education began at the little village school at Obot Idim, not far from his village. Like other children in the neighborhood, Bassey trekked from his village of Ikot Inyang Udo daily to attend classes there. He took and passed some sort of elementary test conducted by the school's proprietors, known as the white priests. They recommended him as a tutor for the local children. Bassey saw a bright future ahead of him as he did the tutoring with much enthusiasm.

The general myth in the village at that time was that whoever went to school and could communicate with the white man would eventually become like him, abandoning his tradition and parents and joining a foreign religion. Because of this negative myth about the white man's education, some parents would not allow their children to go to school. In these families, the only children allowed to attend school were those children who were considered worthless. The beloved children were kept at home and trained so as to take care of their father's property. For this reason, the white man's education was not very popular in Bassey's village. However, he was very positive and eager to learn; therefore no negative myth would stop him from going to school. Moreover, he had no parents who would directly oppose his education. In spite of this myth, he continued his education up to Standard Three, but at that point he was forced to drop out due to financial constraints.

During his school days, Bassey came in contact and fell in love with Catholicism. He wished to be baptized and so submitted himself to take catechism classes in preparation for the baptism. He took these classes for a long time, and when the priests saw that he was ready, he and 3 other candidates trekked to Okon Ikot Essien, a distance of about 20 kilometers, where they were baptized in the Church of St. Joseph on Wednesday, December 13, 1939. At the baptism, in accordance with the Catholic tradition, Bassey took a new name: Mark, after St. Mark the evangelist, one of the synoptic gospel writers.

Whatever prompted Bassey to take that name I do not know, but what I do know very well is that he loved to read and teach the Bible to others. He knew the Bible like the back of his hand. Of course his knowledge was on a layman's level, not that of a Bible scholar. But it was enough to help him do his work perfectly as demanded by his call.

4

Name–Change

As we see in the biblical culture, a change of name always goes with a new mission or a change of destiny. As Fernando Armellini puts it, "God changes the name of a person when he chooses him or her for a special mission."[2] The Lord God Himself personally takes the time to explain the role this new mission comes with, and He shows the need for the change of name. He said this to Abram whom He renamed

---

[2]   Armellini, Fernando. Celebrating the word, vol.1.

Abraham: "No longer shall your name be called Abram, But your name shall be Abraham; for I have made you a father of many nations" (Gen. 17:5). In the case of Sarai whom He re-named Sarah He said: "As for your wife, you are no longer to call her Sarai; her name will be Sarah . . . she shall be a mother of nations and kings of people shall be from her" (Gen.17:15-16). God also said this to Jacob whom He renamed Israel: "Your name will no longer be Jacob, but Israel; for you have struggled with God and with men, and have prevailed" (Gen. 32:28). In the New Testament, Simon was renamed Peter, and Saul was renamed Paul. Based on these biblical examples, at baptism in the Catholic Church we take a new name.

This new name is always the first name, not the last. The case of Bassey Obot was unique; he was also given a new last name. After his baptism, the White Fathers took a special interest in young Bassey, now Mark, because he was able to communicate with them in their language. They listened to his pathetic story of how he lost his parents at the age of six, and how he was struggling to take care of himself from that age including sponsoring himself in school. This story made a very deep impression on the priests, who told him that he was a very special child destined by God to do great things. They let him know that he was a beloved child of God. They also told him that God has become his new parents, and that He had taken care of him in the past and would continue to do so, even more than his parents would. The Fathers therefore changed his last name from Obot, which means creator, to Obot-Ama, which means beloved of the creator. "You are specially loved by God," the priests told him. From then on, Bassey was no longer known as Bassey Obot, but as Mark Obotama—but he kept Bassey as his middle name.

This remained his name for his whole life. He answered to it until July 14, 2002, when on that glorious Sunday morning he was invited by his creator to come for his eternal reward after spending 76 years on earth. Obotama is now a family name which his children and grandchildren all go by. Ever since he was re-named the "beloved of the creator," events in his life consistently bore eloquent testimony to the meaning of this name. In his annals, he had gone from a child without parents to a father of numerous children and grandchildren. This has some semblance to the story of Abraham, our great father in faith. This is the work of the Lord, a marvel in our eyes as the psalmist would love to say.

When I was growing up, I used to hear some elderly paternal relatives call him Okonna. One person who always called him by that name was Mary, his cousin who was married to a man in Okon Ikot Igwe. We used to call her Mary Igwe because surprisingly, her husband's name was also Igwe, just like the name of the village. As to where the name Okonna came from, I have no clue; once again, I did not ask him. It must have been a pet name such as mothers or grandmothers sometimes give to children.

I regret that I did not ask him more questions. I believe this work would have been a lot richer if I had. Papa actually did not promote that name Okonna and did not use it in any of his official documents as far as I know. Most of his documents carry Bassey as a second name after Mark. He so much cherished the name Mark that he did not emphasize the other name. He may have emphasized his baptismal name because he lost his parents at a tender age, and therefore was not so much in touch with the traditional culture as he would have been had his parents lived to influence him more as he was growing up. His parents would probably have called him Bassey for a long time. Because he embraced Christianity at a very young age, that became the culture he identified with and into which he was assimilated, especially as he did not spend a good part of his life in his aboriginal homeland. He imbibed the Christian culture at an age when most of his peers were still being drilled by their parents in the pagan culture, offering pagan sacrifices and celebrating the traditional religious festivals. From a very young age, he was a Catholic and held onto that faith until death. He cut himself off from the pagan culture when he left his village in response to the call of God, just as Abraham did. This symbolized his move away from the traditional culture and towards a new culture—Christianity. Had his parents lived to bring him up to a mature age, would he have been as involved in the Christian culture? That is a matter of conjecture. The creator, however, has His own way of working out people's destiny for a desired result. Catechist Mark Obotama is a solid example of the hand of God leading someone to a desired destiny. His history will always remain a lesson in God's loving care.

5

His Odyssey

The newly-christened Mark Bassey Obotama was very sure he had a bright future ahead of him, and he also knew it could not be realized there in the village of Ikot Inyang Udo. So what could he do about this? He did what many young men of this present generation would do—emigrate. This was not common in those days, but the God who directed his ways showed him the way. At the age of 20, he left his village for Obom Itiat in the present day Itu Local Government Area of Akwa Ibom State, in search of greener pastures. He was not sure what he would do there, but like Abraham, God led him to a job as a station teacher. He enjoyed this job; he had developed a passion for teaching when he was given the tutoring position at his local school. At a time when teachers were scarce, he worked overtime to teach the people catechism. He also acted as an interpreter to the white missionaries who were in the area.

His ministry there was short-lived due to health reasons. Unfortunately, he fell ill at the place of his catechetical work, and his illness was so severe that he could not even trace his way back home. But God's providence was at hand, as was so often the case with him. When you are a "beloved of the creator," He opens ways for you at every point and makes assistance available where human hands cannot. As he lost hope of ever getting back to his village due to the sickness, God sent him a guardian angel in the person of Mr. Alphonsus Mendie from Nto Eton, which is in the present day Obot Akara Local Government Area of Akwa Ibom State, Nigeria. This man was the late father of Rev. Fr. Michael Mendie. He took care of Obotama briefly, and then traced a way to his village of Ikot Inyang Udo, where he dropped him off. That was how his ministry got cut short. As much as he enjoyed it, it turned out that God had another plan for him.

Life may be full of ups and downs, but the one who is in the care of God will always remain stable. The one who fears the Lord has the assurance as the psalmist says, "The angel of the Lord is encamped around those who fear Him to deliver them" (Ps. 34:7). This played out in his life as we shall see. This was just the beginning of his odyssey.

Back in his village, since there was no one to care for him, he abandoned himself to fate and awaited death which he thought was soon coming. It was at this point, when he was almost at the brink of the grave, that he remembered there were some missionary Sisters at Urua Akpan, some distance away from his village. He had a strong sense that they could help him. So powered by instinct of survival, he literally crawled to Urua Akpan to meet the Medical Missionaries of Mary (MMM) Sisters who were there to help the likes of him. On seeing him, the Sisters took pity on him and to their surprise and excitement, he was able to communicate with them in English, which was not common in those days. This was an added impetus to the sisters. They gave him the medical attention he needed at that moment, and he stayed with them in the hospital until he was well enough to go back home and only visit the hospital on alternate days. When they discharged him, they instructed him to eat meat and a lot of vegetables which would provide the nutrients he needed to build up his system.

When he arrived home and told some of his relatives about his experience in the hospital with the Sisters, and that he was told to eat meat, they ridiculed him. This is understandable because meat was not commonly available at that time; even those who were considered upper-class rarely ate meat. How then would an orphan who could barely manage to eat his meals afford the luxury of meat? In his words, "they all laughed at me." He was, however, able to take care of this problem by his usual method of fetching mfang oko and selling them—this time at Urua Akpan market. He would sell them for a few coins and then go to the butcher's booth and offered a little money for the discarded bones which were to be thrown away. The butcher would pack up a great deal for him. These bones were good enough for an orphan who could not afford meat. He was able to cook these bones and just drink the broth. It worked out for him according to his belief—his body constitution responded and he started to gain back his health. When he went back to the Sisters, they were so delighted to see the rapid improvement in his health that they offered him a job. He was asked to perform some menial jobs for them for a wage of one shilling a month. This was enough to keep him going until he moved away from his village to live at Urua Akpan—a place he called home until his death.

He started a new trade, setting up a kiosk close to the hospital where he prepared coffee, tea, and bread for the patients who came to the hospital for treatment from outside the locality. With tea and bread in the morning and some food in the afternoon, he catered to the patients and their families. The response was tremendous, and his business started to grow. It was a blessing when the business turned out to be much more than he expected. It became a popular gathering place for the visiting patients and their families, as well as the local folks.

One fateful evening as he was working in his kiosk, a man walked in whom he thought was a customer, but the man did not order anything. Instead, he sat there quietly for close to 10 minutes, and to an up-and-coming businessman, 10 minutes is a pretty long time. He applied some elementary public relations techniques and engaged the visitor in some conversation. As the conversation went on, he served the visitor a cup of tea and a slice of bread. This little gesture resulted in much more than he could ever have imagined.

The guest asked how much the tea and the slice of bread would cost. Ette Mark—for that was what Obotama had come to be known in the area—told him that it was just his token of appreciation for the visit. The man, who introduced himself as Udo Akpan Ekanem from Ikot Ada Uto, commented that the little booth he was using for the business was not good enough for all the customers coming in to eat. He suggested that Ette Mark needed a permanent place for the business, where he could build a bigger accommodation. Ette Mark told him he had no place to erect a permanent structure. Then Udo Akpan Ekanem told him he could offer him a piece of his own land, just at the periphery of the market, if he had some money. That sounded like a good deal for Ette Mark who readily agreed to get it. They were able to strike a business deal and after the necessary protocols according to local law and custom, including the writing of an agreement, the land was sold to Ette Mark, who then moved out from the little market booth to a permanent place where he operated his restaurant business in full scale. His immediate family still resides on this land today.

Ette Mark was blessed with a booming business; it grew to the point that he had more customers than he could handle alone, so he had to employ some young boys as stewards. As the business bloomed even more, he had to purchase foodstuff from markets outside of the area, so he purchased a bicycle to make the necessary trips. This meant he had to leave the restaurant in the hands of these youngsters for several hours at a time.

Name recognition is magical in the business world. As it turned out, Ette Mark was gradually becoming a well-known name in the restaurant business, and his once-small bread and tea stand was becoming more demanding. He needed a helping hand that was more mature than these young boys, and that was when he started thinking seriously of getting "a helpmate fitting for him." (Gen. 2:18). This would be a better investment than simply hiring helpers. Having been in the area for quite a while, he was starting to put down roots, and he now knew some of the local people. Once again, Papa's story can be compared to that of Abraham, whom the Lord "uprooted" from his aboriginal homeland and "planted" in a strange land where he grew and multiplied. Ette Mark had been planted in a land where he never imagined he could live and work, but by shear providence he was now becoming a household name in catering. Many people young and old would just stroll into the booth to enjoy themselves and relax, mostly in the evenings. He did not need a business name and signpost to advertise his business—the Lord was his advertiser.

6

A Family Man, Teacher, and Catechist

"As for me and my household, we shall serve the Lord."

Joshua 24:15

The divine architect, God the creator, ordained from the beginning of time that a man should have a family when He said, "It is not good that man should be alone. I will make for him a helpmate suitable for him" (Gen. 2:18). He then created Eve and gave her to Adam, and He gave them authority to procreate. This authority is expressed in the divine commission to man to be fruitful and multiply and fill the earth—"be fruitful and multiply and filled the earth" (Gen. 1:28). Every living person must obey this natural law unless it is voluntarily given up, as in the case of celibates for religious reasons. In many cultures, deciding when to start a family rests on the individual. There are, however, certain determinants such as social or economic expediencies that may expedite the need to start a family some times earlier. In Ette Mark's case, his economic expediency determined that he start a family earlier than he would probably have wanted to.

Ette Mark started making a few friends after he had been in the area for a while, but he still did not know a lot of families in the area. Therefore, he had to rely on the directives of his few friends who were natives and knew the local people very well. The first young woman who was introduced to him seemed like the one who would be his wife, but it was not to be according to a very grand design.

He had made some plans to see the family of his would-be bride according to the traditional inquiry program required by native law and custom. He was just planning as a human being, but God had His own plan for him. The night before the inquiry, there was an incident that changed the course of history for him.

He had filled the earthenware pot traditionally known as *Abang Ukot* with palm wine, which was one of the required items in the traditional inquiry package. Just of its own accord, the pot burst and the contents were spilt completely. Ette Mark was upset, but being a very spiritually sensitive person, he saw this as a great sign from God—what other people would call an omen. He prayed about it and called off the inquiry. The family, whose name I will not mention here, was understandably upset.

Nonetheless, it was still very necessary for Ette Mark to have a lasting helpmate. So he approached another of his very close friends from Ikot Ada Uto, Sam Nwoko, or as the local people used to call him, "Asam Anwoko." Ette Mark asked him to help him find a good girl for him to marry. He confided to Sam that he needed a person who could take care of the business when he went on his necessary trips to purchase items from distant markets. By all traditional standards he was considered ready: he had a bicycle, he had a house, and he had enough money to take care of himself and a wife.

It did not take Sam long to come back with a report. He had seen a young and industrious girl from Idung Okoro in Ikot Ada Uto. She used to pass by his compound on her way to and from *Aworoto* (to be candid, I don't know what this name means and none of those I have asked knows either), the local pond that served as a water source for the locality. This was and still remains a small pond with some little cisterns dug in the ground to fetch water. Sam told him about this girl who, according to him, would make a good housewife judging from the way she was taking care of her siblings in spite of her young age. On hearing this report about her, Ette Mark was satisfied with her qualities and told Sam to make further inquiries about this girl, and then, in his usual style, he prayed about it.

All of his inquiries about her came back with positive answers. So Ette Mark set out on a mission to see this girl in person. He saw her and was satisfied. Preliminary nuptial inquiries were conducted according to native law and custom. The traditional marriage was contracted and the girl became his wife. God indeed has a strange way of designing destinies. His ways often amaze us humans, as happened here in the coming together of this new couple.

These two strangers brought together by God had certain things in common. They were both similar in many ways, which was one of the reasons they were compatible with one another. The young girl in question was Anna John Udoh, to whom Ette Mark gave the pet name of "Mmayen." She is the present-day Mrs. Margaret Mark Obotama, the mother of 7 children and grandmother of 23 grandchildren, fondly called Mma Obot by many people in the vicinity.

Anna John lost her mother, Mma Elisabeth Udoh, at the age of fourteen. Unlike the husband who grew up taking care only of himself, she had some siblings behind her that she was required by custom to look after, being the eldest in the polygamous family of Chief John Udoh. But they both grew up shouldering adult responsibilities at young ages due to early loss of parents. These circumstances of their early lives influenced their approach to life and their general world view. When she was approached for her hand in marriage, her greatest concern was what to do with her four siblings, three boys and one girl, the youngest of which was not yet three years old and for whom she had become "mother." Anna John was blessed that the man who wanted her hand in marriage was ready to take care of the siblings also. They all moved into the marital home of their senior sister when she became a housewife. The couple was taking care of four children before they even had their first child.

Anna John's siblings lived with her in her marital home until they were all grown up. Unfortunately, only one of those four siblings is still alive today. She is also a mother and grandmother now. The three boys have all passed on. Two were killed in the Nigerian/ Biafran war while fighting on the Biafran side, and the youngest died as a result of a workplace accident in Port Harcourt, Rivers State where he was searching for his daily bread.

The beginning of their married life was not an easy ride; the couple had more mouths to feed than the resources at their disposal would allow. It was a lot of struggle trying to make ends meet. As God would have it, the restaurant business thrived, but even then they had barely enough to take care of themselves. But they did not give up. Every Edet market day—one of the local market days—which was and still is the most important market day in the area, they were very busy preparing food, because they usually had a lot of customers that day. The whole locality would come to the market that day, and they would purchase a lot of things wholesale because merchants came in from the neighboring cities of Aba in Abia State and Ikot Ekpene in Akwa Ibom State. They would spend some time purchasing all they would need in the coming days.

Ette Mark and his wife needed to make purchases as well, so at a certain time during the day, they would close the restaurant and go into the market. When Ette Mark purchased, his young wife would carry the items to the house. On one of these market days, they were doing this as usual, but at one point his wife had gone to drop off the purchased items at home and did not return for a long time. After waiting for close to an hour, he suspected that something must have happened. He went to the house to find out what must have delayed her all this time, and when he arrived, there in front of the house were the items he had purchased an hour earlier. They were just lying there, and the doors were still locked and there was nobody to say where his wife had gone with the keys. The children in the house were normally sent home a day before Edet market day, since the restaurant was only opened for half a day. As he stood there, trying to make sense of the scene playing out before him, somebody came and told him that his wife had been taken away by the priests.

Ette Mark knew immediately why his wife had been "arrested" by the priests. They were not formally wedded in the church, but were just living together. He knew he should go to the parish church to see the priests. He left immediately, and at the parish center he was told that his wife was in the marriage quarters—a mission house where women stay while undergoing tutoring as they prepare for marriage, but he was prevented from seeing her. Later in the day he went back with some food for her. She remained in the marriage quarters for three weeks, undergoing marriage instructions.

On Wednesday, March 21, 1956, Ette Mark was joined in holy matrimony to Miss Anna John Udoh of Ikot Ada Uto. Rev. Fr. Fitzgerald received their consent in St. Bridget's Parish Church, Urua Akpan. Given Ette Mark's personal history, one can imagine that this was not a high-class wedding. There was no bridal train, no photographers, no wedding gown, and no reception after the wedding. He simply carried his new bride on his bicycle and rode her back home. It was as simple as the word simple. That set the stage for the simple family life that goes on even now.

Ette Mark was a simple man all his life. His joy on that wedding day was not because of any party or elaborate reception, but because he could return to the Eucharist which he had not been allowed to receive until after the wedding. He could not even recall any special dish they had that day to mark the wedding. In human reckoning, the day simply rolled away unnoticed; but in the eyes of the creator, a happy and blessed family was set into motion.

The beginning of their life as a couple was not rosy. They really experienced hard times, but they remained hopeful. They were a couple who literally shared everything, even clothing. As Mama always told us when we were growing up, she had just one good wrapper and this was what she wore to church, and the husband had just one shirt and one pair of shorts. Such a life would be difficult for the present generation of couples who would find it hard to cope, but for Papa, who had been a teacher, this was just a way he could teach married couples today in practical terms. Riches do not make a happy marriage; love and understanding do. So Ette Mark did not just teach from the Bible and the catechism, but from his own life experience. In fact, one of the reasons I am writing this book is so that people who read it will learn something from his life.

Ultimately, it was the grace of God that really propelled them on. This can come to any couple who submit themselves to the grace of God.

Shortly after the wedding, Ette Mark was offered a job as a station teacher by the parish priest. He was posted to Ikot Essien station in the present day Okon Parish by Rev. Fr. Thomas Greeley, who was the parish priest and manager of schools at the time. (Modern readers may not know that schools at that time were managed by the Church, and the priests were in charge of the schools). Due to this new job, Ette Mark had to discontinue the restaurant business in order to move to his new assignment at Ikot Essien, Okon. At that time, what is now known as Okon Parish was under Urua Akpan Parish. At Ikot Essien, he worked both as a school teacher and what today would be known in our diocese as a Station Catechist, teaching in the school and conducting morning prayers on weekdays and Sunday services in the Church. This was the way the system worked in the days when the schools were known as Mission Schools, and were under the administration of the Catholic Church.

A landmark event in the life of the young couple took place in early 1957. Ette Mark was still at Ikot Essien at that time, 39 days into the New Year and eleven months into their married life. On Friday morning, February 8, 1957, in the birth suite of St. Mary's hospital in Urua Akpan, I was born. A new chapter was opened in the history of the young couple as they became parents.

When the good news was announced to my father who was anxiously waiting outside the birth suite, he came into the unit (when it was appropriate) and lifted me with both hands. He raised me up above his head and sang *Itoro Abasi K'enyong,* the vernacular version of "Praise to the Holiest in the Heights," much to the admiration of all the nurses and other mothers in the unit. He then put a writing pen into my tiny clinched fist, which I held until late afternoon of that day.

If anyone asks me why he gave me that writing pen, I can only give an educated guess—maybe he wanted me to be an educated person or better still, a writer or journalist. But these are just guesses. I regret that I did not actually ask him what the symbolism of that ritual was. However, I can guess from the sentiments expressed by one of my father's surviving relatives when we visited him at Ikot Inyang Udo, when I must have been about four years old and my brother Paul was about three. He said to us that we were the hope of the family. "You will achieve academic prowess that we were not able to, due to ignorance. You are our hope." That statement did not have any meaning to me at that moment. I was just a little child, but I can still remember just running around the house until Papa invited us inside for prayers with him. After the prayers, which were for our paternal relative, we left and that was the last time we saw him alive. He died a short while later and we went for the funeral.

On the day I was installed as an acolyte in the winter of 1984, a male cousin from my paternal side, Mr. Akpan Jimmy Akpan, gave me a pen. It was then that Papa made a comment about giving me a pen on the day I was born. Though Bro-Akpan was not aware of it, when he gave me a pen on that day when I took my first step toward the completion of my priestly journey, it was as though he was repeating what Papa had done on the day of my birth.

The fact that I was born when Papa was at Ikot Essien fostered a special affinity between Papa and the people of Ikot Essien Station. He was baptized at Ikot Essien and his first official appointment as a station teacher was to Ikot Essien. Papa always tried to maintain that relationship. I can still remember at the christening of my sister Uduak, the choir from Ikot Essien Catholic Station came to Urua Akpan to sing at the Mass. Their performance that day made a very deep impression on the people of Urua Akpan. On the day I celebrated my second Thanksgiving Mass at my home Station, St. Paul's Catholic Church Midim Atan, the people of Ikot Essien Station came and gave me, among many other things, a very symbolic gift: a coconut seedling, with a special instruction that it be planted as a historical plant from Ikot Essien Church. At Papa's funeral, a large number of Ikot Essien people came to bid him farewell. St. Joseph's Parish—Okon, presented a condolence message to our family. (see appendix)

My kid brother, Rev. Fr. Lawrence Obotama, has a very special friend who is a priest from Ikot Essien station, Rev. Fr. Linus Ebere. He honored my brother with an invitation to preach at his second Thanksgiving Mass at Ikot Essien Station. Which he did to the satisfaction of everybody in the church that day.

Papa always wanted to provide opportunity for us to learn, be it within or outside of the classroom. When he was younger and full of vitality, he would take us around to see things he considered educational. A good example readily comes to mind—I must not have been more than three years old and my brother Paul was just a little baby. Papa took us on a sightseeing trip with Mama to a site in our village where the Shell Company had just discovered some mineral deposits in the swamps of our little stream at Ikot Inyang Udo. It was quite a sight to see. Being so young, I could only watch and wonder about those big machines that I saw. There were also some big tanks and giant drilling rigs, and a huge hose was running on the ground with some liquid flowing from it into those giant tanks. There were huge generators that were steaming, and in a short distance were tarpaulin tents. Nobody was there to explain to us what all those were and there was no explanation of what was going on here. All the explanation we had was from the local people, who trooped there every day from the surrounding villages. From as far away as Okon, it was understood that the Shell Company was drilling oil—*erok aran*. In my very tender mind I wondered what all that meant, because the only oil I knew was the one my mom used for domestic purposes. And that oil did not look anything like this.

Another puzzling thing was the white people at the site. In my infantile mind, I thought that every white man was a priest; but the ones we saw here were not as neat as the white men in our parish. These looked dirty in their work-suits. They were living in tarpaulin tents, not in buildings as our priests in the mission were. I was so confused as to why white men would live that way. So on our bicycle ride back to Urua Akpan, I had several questions for Papa.

He provided answers to all the questions I asked him. Whether they were correct I did not know, but he satisfied my curiosity and as far as I was concerned, Papa knew everything. He explained the difference between the oil that is drilled underneath the earth and the one Mama prepares from palm fruits and uses for cooking. He also took time to explain to me that not all white people are priests, just like not all priests are white. I was shocked to hear that for the first time. In my mind, priests were specifically designed to have white skins, and once somebody became a priest, I thought God changed him and gave him a white skin to look like those holy images I used to see in pictures depicting the saints. I had never seen a black priest; I didn't think that a black person could be a priest, and I could not even imagine a priest in a black skin. My imaginative impression was fueled by one boy whose name I have forgotten, but he was from Ikot Ukpong Offiong, a neighboring village. He was one of the altar boys at that time and he had a light skin, and I thought that he was in the process of becoming a priest. That was how far my naive imagination could take me.

That evening, while Mama was preparing dinner, Papa took time to lecture me on the different races of people. The priests came from a country where everybody was white. That was another startling revelation to me. I was trying to imagine a village where everybody was white. I was wondering if that could even exist in this world, because my own world was just within Urua Akpan and its environs.

After the "lecture" on the white race that evening, I'm not very sure whether I really concentrated the following morning at Mass (even though children rarely concentrate at Mass anyway). I was just focusing on the white priests and trying to imagine a "village" where everybody was white and there were no black people. The way Papa explained the ethnicity of the white race really raised my curiosity, although today that explanation would be very offensive to some orthodox Africanists. He made me believe that they knew everything, and that Jesus was a white man. He went on and on, extolling the superiority of the white race and all other Eurocentric doctrines that I don't feel comfortable writing down here. But to be fair to Papa, I have to exonerate him for that because he was just presenting the white image as he was taught to believe. The priest was the epitome of that superiority doctrine. Everything that came from a priest was like a word from God. Papa could never imagine arguing with a priest, even if he happened to know that what the priest said was not exactly correct. To argue with a priest would be like arguing with God. In his personal belief, the person closest to God was the priest. Though Papa had not been trained as a theologian, he was able to present to us the church's teaching on the priests as the Alter Christus—another Christ; a teaching he tried to instill in all of us his children and grandchildren. A priest must be obeyed no matter what, for God's wrath always awaited whoever disobeyed a priest. He maintained his belief in the trustworthiness of priests until his death.

A good number of my siblings still hold to this doctrine till today, even though there are two priests in the family at the time of writing of this book. Papa was a very respectful person, and one of the very important teachings he left with us was that no one should ever argue with an elderly person. That concept has had a significant impact on our family life, and sometimes I even wonder if it was a good teaching or not.

After he married an indigene of Ikot Ada Uto and lived there for a long time, Papa started getting involved with the socio-cultural life of the local people. He assimilated their culture, and being an in-law, he could join in their social life. He started contributing to the village and got used to the people. At the time we were growing up, the only village we could associate and identify with was Ikot Ada Uto. Papa's bride's relatives became his "new family." He even called his father in-law, our grandfather, "Papa," as if he were his biological father. This showed the relationship he had with his bride's family. He seemed to have found solace in this family, who made up for the family he did not have back in his aboriginal home.

In our primary school days, I used to introduce myself as coming from Ikot Ada Uto. We got used to the people there, because this was the group of people we could identify with. It was after the Nigerian/ Biafra civil war that we had a serious relationship with the people of Ikot Inyang Udo, our aboriginal home.

As Papa was always serving in other parishes, he rarely had time for farm work which was and is very essential in the life of our people. The masculine aspect of farming required his presence; so he got some people to help. I can remember some of them, such as Idio Akpan Adia-Ekpe and Etim Lazarus from Ikot Ada Uto. They were in their early twenties, and were always on hand to help when Papa was away in the station, as we used to call the parish or school where Papa used to work. Once Etim took us to go visit Papa in one of the stations—I think it was Ikot Essien in Okon.

One of the masculine jobs they helped with was the first harvest of yams, which is time-sensitive. When the farming season came around, they were always available to accompany Papa through the different stages of the farming, clearing, and planting of the seed yams. At harvest times they also came around to help. When I was gathering information for this book, I spoke with Mama on the phone and asked her about them. Unfortunately, the two of them have passed on, God rest them, but their families are still keeping in touch with our family. They do visit our family during some festivals like Christmas and special family events.

In 1963, Papa was transferred to St. Charles School Ukana Uwa West, where he also doubled as a teacher/Station Catechist. At Ukana Uwa I was about six years old, and I attended the primary school there. My brother Paul, my late uncle Joseph John (whom we used to call by his vernacular name, Effiong), and I were living with Papa. Every morning he would wake us up for prayers, and then he would leave to the school block which also served as the station church in front of the teacher's house where we lived, to conduct morning prayers while we prepared for school. He was there for about two years before he was inducted into the catechetical ministry of the diocese as a diocesan catechist. This was in 1965, the bishop of Ikot Ekpene diocese at that time, Most Rev. Dominic I. Ekandem (who later became Dominic Cardinal Ekanem, of blessed memory) saw the need to have diocesan catechists that could be posted to parishes outside their home parishes to work with priests. This helped to boost the lay ministry, because the catechists are closer to the lay faithful than the priests. Papa was blessed to be among the first batch of diocesan catechists. He was posted to Urua Inyang Parish but was residing at Ikot Udom station (now a parish), where there was a station house. We went with him and we were attending the primary school at Ikot Ebenwang. Papa's stay in Urua Inyang was brief; in 1966, he was transferred to Inen Parish under the parish priest, Rev. Fr. P. Walsh of blessed memory. Papa served as the first parish catechist there.

When he was at Inen Parish, tragedy struck our family. My sister, Rose Mark Obotama, died at the tender age of four. The night she passed was a tense night that I will never, ever forget. It was very traumatic for every one of us in the family. That was the first time in my life that I saw my parents cry.

Rose was the third child and the first female in the birth order of the family. She was sick for just a few days, and Mama took her to the hospital according to our family practice and she was admitted. We thought she would come back after a few days. Marcus was just a little baby then. I can't remember very well whether Mama sent for Papa at Inen or if he just came by mere instinct, or if it was one of those times when he was attending a diocesan meeting at Ifuho and would come home to spend the night before returning to Inen the following day. What I do remember well was that when Papa arrived, he went straight to the hospital and was directed to the ward where Rose was. She was still receiving intravenous fluids, and Mama was there in the hospital with her. Little Marcus, whom Papa had nick-named Koko-Ette, was left at home with my aunt, Josephine, who was part of our family and was the primary baby-sitter. She took him to the hospital regularly, because Mama thought it was not safe for him to remain in the hospital with her.

When Papa arrived, Mama briefed him on what happened. He stayed with us longer than usual because of the sickness, and he stayed with us while Mama was in the hospital with Rose. On that fateful night, we finished our night rosary and went to bed. Papa was still praying—it must have been about two or three in the morning—when there was a knock on the front door of our house. This knock woke all of us up. Papa went and opened the door.

There stood the man called "Ette Willie" from Ikot Ada Uto. He was the hospital night-gateman. He talked to Papa in a very low tone. We heard Papa exclaim, "Oh Mark!" He kept repeating that while he went into the bedroom and changed out of his night clothes, and then he changed from "Oh Mark" to "Jesus tua mi mbom, Mary nnyanga mi"—"Jesus have mercy on me, Mary help me." We suspected something had happened but we did not have the courage to ask him. Ette Willie had since returned to the hospital which was just several yards away from our house. Papa asked Nnwa (Josephine), who was the eldest among us, to lock the door and watch over us. As he stepped out into the night with a lantern in his hand, he kept repeating, "Jesus tua mi mbom, Mary nnyanga mi."

We were all wondering what must have happened in the hospital to warrant the gateman to come and call Papa. Our juvenile minds did not comprehend that something tragic had happened. In about forty minutes the answer to all our questions came when we heard somebody wailing right from the hospital gate. As soon as we recognized it as Mama's voice, we knew that the news was bad. We had lost our sister.

Simultaneously, Effiong (my uncle) and Nnwa (my aunt) started crying and we all joined before Mama could even reach the house. In just a few minutes there was a knock on the door and Nnwa opened while we were still crying. There were several people in front of our house, and Mama had thrown herself down and was rolling in the puddle left by the previous day's rainfall. There was pandemonium in the entire house as Papa walked in and calmly dropped the lifeless body of our lovely sister Rose on the bed in the parlor (living room). Within a few minutes, the entire neighborhood had gathered in our house, and some people were standing outside. Everybody was crying; Rose was so loved by the entire neighborhood because of her beauty. Papa went out and tried to bring Mama in, and with some help from the men of the neighborhood they brought her inside.

As Papa walked in, he noticed some droplets of sweat on Rose's forehead and the body was warm, so he called out her name three or four times and shook her; but there was no response. That was when Papa could not control himself anymore. He sat down on the bare floor and cried. Our sister Rose had truly passed on.

It was the most traumatic thing in my life to see my father cry. I regarded him as the strongest person I had ever known. I do not know whether the sight of my father crying or the death of my sister was the more traumatic. The site of Papa crying intensified our wailing as we rolled on the ground. By daybreak, my grandfather and many of my maternal relatives had arrived from Idung Okoro. It was an emotionally-charged night, the kind of night I would not wish to see again in my life time.

That morning, Papa did not go for morning Mass, but after Mass one of the priests came and consoled my parents. Mama was so difficult to console.

Later that morning, at about 9 am, the Parish Priest, Rev. Fr. T. Greeley came and performed the funeral rite and buried our little sister Rose. During the interment, as the priest was praying and we were still crying, an elderly neighbor of ours told us to stop crying because the priest was giving our sister directions to heaven. She said if we continued to cry, she may not hear the directions and could miss her way. We certainly did not want that, so we all kept quiet immediately because we wanted her to reach heaven safely. I know now that she was just trying to keep us calm, and she succeeded.

Papa was at the grave side, and tried to brave it as a man; but Mama was inside the house crying. After the funeral, a lot of people kept coming to our house on condolence visits. Almost every person who came in to console my parents would hear Papa saying "Abasi okono, Abasi obo edidiong enyene enying obong"—"The Lord gave, the Lord has taken away, blessed be the name of the Lord."

It was only when I went to the seminary several years later that I knew he had been quoting the words from the book of Job. Papa was very good at citing the scriptures, and he wouldn't hesitate to correct you if you messed up with the citation. I remember once when I was still in the minor seminary, one of my friends came to visit me and spent the night with my family. The following morning he joined us at our family morning prayers. I was supposed to give a reflection that morning and cited a wrong verse of scripture. Despite the presence of my friend, Papa corrected me immediately after the morning prayers. After that, I and my other siblings made sure to take time to study the scripture.

After the funeral, Papa arranged to take the whole family back to Inen so as to help Mama recover from the shock of Rose's death. At Inen, Papa sent her to learn how to bake bread with Mr. Moses Umoh, the brother of Rev. Fr. Dominic Umoh. The rigor of that trade was enough to take her mind from the death of Rose.

In the spring of the following year, my sister Maria was born and Papa named her "Idong-Esit"—consolation. This name has since lost out to her baptismal name, Maria. Not many people in the family even remember that name now. Even if some of us remember, it does not carry much weight.

Inen Parish then comprised of three big sections, Inen, Asakpa and Ekparakwa. Asakpa and Ekparakwa have since become parishes. Papa lived and worked in those three sections consecutively while they were still under Inen Parish. He stayed briefly at Inen and moved to Ikot Etim, which was a connecting point for Asakpa section then. Ikot Etim has since become a parish also. When we were there with Papa, Effiong, Paul, and I attended St. Michael's Primary School, Ikot Etim, even though we resided in a house at Ikot Andem. Later he moved to Ekparakwa.

One particular day in that school stands out in my mind, and that was Monday, June 6, 1966. One of our classmates, I can't remember his name now, called our attention to the date. We were excited about it as we wrote on our notebooks, 6-6-66. Nothing significant happened on that day, but I recall the excitement we all had over the numbers in the date.

Once again, we did not spend a long time in that school, because Papa had to send Paul and I back to Urua Akpan to continue our studies, leaving Effiong to stay with him at Ikot Etim. The decision this time had nothing to do with Papa's transfer, but rather a little squabble I had with one of the teachers. Once again, I am choosing to withhold his name; but I still remember his name even now, and the incident is still very fresh in my memory as if it happened yesterday.

There was a certain levy called the sports fund into which every pupil was asked to pay three pence. Of course, three pence was a fat sum of money in 1966. We could not pay on the scheduled day, but a day of grace was given to those of us who could not pay. About three days after the deadline had expired, the few people who had not paid were called out in the assembly, and the teacher who was in charge of sports asked who among us was sure he/she would pay the following day. If someone was sure of this, he could join the rest of the pupils. Everybody went in except me.

Even Effiong, who of course was my senior in age, had joined the other group and was beckoning on me to come. I did not, because in my mind I knew there was no way I would be able to pay the money the following day. Papa was in one of the out stations conducting retreat and was not expected back until Sunday. I thought that if I joined the group, I would be lying, and I did not want that.

The teacher did not ask me why I would not pay the next day. Instead, he insulted Papa for not giving me the money, and said how the catechists were always reporting the teachers to the priests for a reward of some eggs. He said this in the presence of the whole school. As little as I was, I was so embarrassed I started crying. The embarrassment was too much, so I decided to do something I would not ordinarily have done—report it to Papa on his return.

When Papa came back, I reported the case to him, and he came to the school and tendered a complaint with the headmaster. At that time, schools were still under the mission and the headmaster knew what the consequence would be if the priest heard about the case. He pleaded with Papa not to take any action. He promised to handle the case himself. When the teacher in question was summoned to the headmaster's office, he denied ever saying that. For fear of victimization, Papa decided to withdraw us from that school.

It was here at Asakpa section that Papa chased away some workers from their farm. He was returning from one of the out-stations on his motorbike one Sunday. The bishop then, who later became Cardinal Ekandem, bought those motorbikes for the first batch of catechists he commissioned in the diocese. Papa used to ride on that to visit the stations, so when the workers saw him, they thought he was a government official, because motorbikes were not common that time. So before he even got to them, they all ran away. He stood there and yelled at them to stop working on Sunday and go to church.

In 1967, Papa moved to Ekparakwa. His stay in Ekparakwa was truncated by the breakout of the Nigerian/Biafra civil war, when he had to return home to Urua Akpan to be with his family. War time was another threatening period for every person living in the two conflicting nations, but mostly for those on the Biafran side. The civil war years were the first time we had all lived together as a family for a long time. Papa's profession demanded that he moved from one parish to another. Mama was always at home with the rest of the family, which was not very large at that time. These war years helped us develop as a family with both parents on the watch.

The civil war changed the history of every living person within the geographical space that was carved out and formed into Biafra. There was a literal stagnation for everybody, and in most cases there was a return to family roots as people fled their places of work and joined their kin at home. Catechist Obotama returned to his base at Urua Akpan, and being such a workaholic when it came to religious activities, it did not take long before he resumed his catechetical duties there. He helped instruct couples preparing for marriage, and performed other services of a catechist.

As the war stretched on, the Biafran government reopened schools which had shut down unofficially as people deserted their homes. When the first bomb was dropped in Urua Akpan by the Nigerian airforce, everybody deserted the place and the primary school shut down. Papa was lucky to be among those employed to teach the young children in these newly reopened schools, many of whom were children of the war refugees. He was assigned to teach at the primary school in Ikot Ukpong Etor. Since they taught under extraordinary circumstances, everything was unconventional. Instead of salaries they were given food supplies, which in war-time parlance were known as "ration." Every other week, all the teachers from the different schools came to Urua Akpan to collect their food ration, because Urua Akpan was a distributing center for two International charity organizations called Caritas International and World Council of Churches.

When Papa was teaching at Ikot Ukpong Etor, my sister Etiido was born in 1969. She is now married and living there in Ikot Ukpong Etor coincidentally.

The war brought about a lot of improvised and extraordinary situations. A case in point was when the first bomb was dropped at Urua Akpan, and we all evacuated the place and took refuge at Ikot Igwe in the compound of one of our extended relatives. Our stay there extended to the Holy Week of that year, and

Papa did not want to let the Holy Week pass without marking it. Here's where it gets extraordinary: Papa became an un-official chief celebrant of the Holy Week liturgy.

Papa arranged for us to have a little Palm Sunday service in the compound where we resided. We had palm branches, even though they were not blessed, and we sang some songs and had a procession around the house where we lived. Papa did some readings because as at that time, he was the only person who could read. We were kids. It was a make-do service, but it fulfilled the Palm Sunday obligation for that year. He delivered a sermon—of course he was good at that.

Throughout the Triduum he became our unofficial chief celebrant as we marked each of the three days with readings, prayers, and songs. One thing about Papa—he never joked with prayers and with the liturgy. Looking back now I can really appreciate him for who he was, which I did not really appreciate at that time, of course as a kid you view things differently. Papa was ready to express his faith publicly if occasion demanded it.

I can remember another incident that occurred during the war. We had left Ikot Igwe and were living at Ikot Obong in the compound where our maternal aunt was married. One of the residents of the compound just collapsed, and everybody panicked. Papa went to him as he was struggling on the ground, and asked if he would like to be baptized. Surprisingly, the patient declined and Papa left the scene immediately, not saying any other word. We followed him. We knew he was disappointed that the person did want to be baptized. I think the person died later.

After the civil war, Papa was posted to Okon Parish as a parish catechist in 1970. He was the first parish catechist of that parish. There was no catechist's house there, so we resided in one of the rooms in the convent school opposite the parish. We resumed our primary school education in St. Joseph's Catholic School Okon. It was at Okon Parish that I cemented my desire to study in seminary. For the first time, I came in close contact with seminarians. They used to come in for meetings with the parish priest, who was then, Rev. Fr. Ephraim S. Obot, who later became a bishop and was posted to Idah. Bishop Obot passed on in 2008. In December of 1970, the seminarians organized some students' activities under the auspices of Okon Students and Ex-Students Association. I remember the drama they presented in which Camillus Etokudoh from Ikot Uko Etor station, now the Lord Bishop of Port Harcourt, acted the part of Isaac while Joseph Udondata played the Esau character. I cannot remember very well who acted the part of Jacob; I think it was either Isidore Uko or Francis Theodore. But it was the Isaac character played by Camillus Etokudoh who caught our attention as kids, because of the way he interpreted that character's role. He practically became the character. The climax of the drama was when the Esau character played by Joseph Udondata discovered that there was no more blessing for him in spite of his pleas with Isaac, his father. Isaac told him that thorns and thistles were on his ways. Meaning he had a curse on his head. The Esau character could not take it any more, and out of frustration he pushed his blind father so hard that he staggered, almost falling down, but still did not open his eyes. He acted the old blind character of Isaac so perfectly that we kids thought he had actually turned blind. I was just beginning my teen years then. After the drama we trooped to their dressing room (which was the parish priest's office) to see what would happen to him, because we thought he really had turned blind. But to our surprise and relief, we saw all the actors laughing at each other including the Isaac charater—Camillus Etokudoh.

Papa must have seen how excited I was running after the actors. In the evening he was talking to us (my brother Paul, Marcus and me) about the way seminarians are trained and how they always perform more than other students from the secular secondary schools. He told us that they were specially trained so that when they became priests they could lead others. He cited the example of the drama we just watched that afternoon, and said that I could do that too if I went to seminary. That was just the encouragement I needed, because I was secretly nursing the idea of going to seminary.

I already admired the way the seminarians were conducting the catechism classes, which were part of their routine when they arrived home for holidays. The seminary uniform was a very attractive, peachpuff-colored, French suit which I admired very much whenever I saw them in it. Then one of our contemporaries, a fellow cub-scout member named Sylvester Ukeh who was just a year ahead of me in the primary school, was admitted into the seminary the following year. At that point, I resolved to go to the seminary at all costs. Of course Papa was very supportive.

He was transferred to Abak in 1973, where he served again under his former parish priest, His Lordship Most Rev. Ephraim Obot of happy memory. That was when I started my studies at Queen of Apostles Seminary—Afaha Obong. I did not have the opportunity to stay with him at Abak, because his stay there was not long. And of course as a seminarian I always went home to help in the home parish.

In 1974, Papa was posted to Midim Parish, where he served under Rev. Fr. Paul Hardy. Here I only visited him twice; the first time was when I was sent out to collect school fees. I spent one weekend at Midim, and then I returned during one of the holidays. Papa was later transferred back to Urua Akpan, where he eventually retired.

Anyone who had the opportunity to be with Papa for any length of time was influenced by him. Anyone who was not influenced by him had a question mark on his or her forehead. This was because Papa was always instructing whoever spent time with him. He was highly influential in a very positive way.

His influence over his children and grandchildren is another testimony to this. He taught in the manner of the apostles, who were uneducated but highly influential through the One who gave them grace. Sometimes you could hear Papa struggling within his limited capacity to explain what even theologians find challenging. I remember how he would struggle to explain the trinity to us in a language that would make sense to us as little kids.

During my theological studies, I appreciated how he had tried in a layman's language to explain some theological facts to us. His legacy lives on in the family and we will try to keep it alive. That was one thing I promised Papa the day I arrived home from the States for his funeral, and my kid brother, Nnabuk (now Fr. Lawrence) took me to where Papa was embalmed. In that room, in the presence of my brother, I spoke to Papa as he was lying there. I told him that I really appreciated all he did for us, and promised him that we will try to keep his legacy going.

Papa was an avid instructor. There are many traditional Catholic hymns in the hymn book that we could sing by heart, courtesy of his training. Sometimes now, when I hear some of these hymns, they evoke some nostalgic feelings. One such hymn is the Christmas carol, "Kop Nte Mm'angel"—"Angels We Have Heard on High." It brings back memories of the times when my brother Paul and me were sitting down while Papa taught us that song some days before Christmas. He explained the meaning of the lyrics to us. Then during Christmas time he would intone that hymn at morning prayers and we (Paul and me) would sing it with gusto.

What made this hymn particularly special was the air of the season, which for us kids was the best time of the year. As Andy Williams sings, "It's the most wonderful time of the year." It was a time for new clothes, rice and stew on that special day, masquerades, and the dry Harmattan winds. All of these together presented a special treat to us kids, and left a deep impression of Christmastime on my psyche. The Christmas of 2002 was especially emotional for me. I was in Detroit, Michigan at that time, and when the choir at St. Stephen/ Mary Mother of Church Parish sang "Angels We Have Heard on High" at the Christmas Day Mass, it aroused a very nostalgic feelings in me. That was the first Christmas after the passing away of my father.

Papa would always correct anything he felt was not done correctly, particularly when it concerned the liturgy. Rev. Fr. Donatus Akpan celebrated his first Mass in St. Bridget's Parish Church, Urua Akpan after his ordination in 1985. I was doing a live commentary of the Mass and I used one particular vernacular proverb. Papa took me up on that, when I arrived home after the function he told me that it was not proper to use a vernacular proverb while doing a commentary at Mass. In our adolescent years we sometimes tried to poke some subtle fun at him whenever he came out with what we used to call his "ultra-conservative doctrines." Of course we only enjoyed that freedom as grown-up kids—I would not have dreamt of doing that when I was still very young.

I remember in my first year in the priesthood, when I was at St. Vincent's Parish Ikot Ekpene which has now been renamed St. Vincent's Parish Ikot Obong Edong, I had a dog which I named Dragon. One day I visited home with the dog, and Mama asked me what the name of the dog was. When I told her it was Dragon, Papa, whom I thought was not paying any attention to our conversation, turned to me immediately and asked me to change that name. When I asked him why, he asked me if I do not read the Bible, because dragons were associated with the evil one and God had cursed the dragon. I made a joke out of it by asking him if I could re-name the dog "St. Paul" since he was associated with evangelism.

"I don't know," he answered. "There are many names you can give to a dog, but not Dragon. You have to change it." I just laughed and that was the end of the conversation. That goes to show the kind of man Papa was.

He was very concerned about the celebration of the liturgy, especially the Holy Sacrifice of the Mass. His entire life was centered on the Eucharist. When I started my life as a young priest, he called me one day and said, "Whenever you celebrate Mass, know that the whole life of the church depends on that. Take time to celebrate it such that even if there is a Protestant in the congregation, he will know that you are doing something important." Papa wanted me to celebrate the Holy Mass with the awe and decorum it deserves. He told me that as a lay person, he could tell if a priest had faith and believed in the Eucharist by the way he celebrates the Mass. He could tell a lot about the faith of the priest by the way he celebrates Mass. Papa reminded me (as if I had forgotten) that the family has faith in nothing but God. I should always demonstrate that faith in my celebration of the Eucharist. I have tried to keep to Papa's teaching in this—saying the rosary and celebrating the Mass are two things I make sure to do every day as long as I remain alive.

One thing that Papa was so good at which I did not appreciate as a little kid growing up was medication. Once he noticed that any of us ran a slight fever, the next thing was that all of us would be on the way to the hospital. Sometimes he would invite one man we used to call "Uko-Ekpe"—I don't know if that was his real name or nickname—to come and give us injections at home. Throughout my young years and even now, I have a phobia for needles. I dreaded injection and anybody associated with it. Uko-Ekpe was one of those I dreaded, and any nurse who had given me an injection in the hospital. Uko-Ekpe used to ride on a bicycle carrying his wooden box containing the medications and all of his very small-scale medical equipment. Each time he appeared we would be nervous. Any time one of us had a fever, we all would be watching out, and at the sound of a bicycle bell outside—usually in the evening after market—we would dash out to see if it was he. His visits always sent cold fear down our spines. Uko-Ekpe became our nemesis.

Sometimes Papa would carry me on his bicycle to the dispensary at Central Annang county headquarters (which has now become the headquarters of Essien Udim Local Government) for treatment. Sometimes we would leave before breakfast and spend close to an hour there, which for a young child seemed like eternity. Papa was very serious when it came to our health. One thing you would always see in our house was medicine. No wonder so many members of my family are medical practitioners—Paul and his wife Anne, Marcus and his wife Itoro and Sr. Maria. We did not use herbs as at that time—only on a very few occasions were we given some traditional herbs. Our whole healthcare was centered on scientific medication. My siblings who have kids now train them that way.

Papa's spirituality was on a very high frequency, and anybody who came in contact with him had no doubt about this. His spirituality knew no bounds; it cut across all spheres of life. He saw the mind of God in almost everything, and that made him to do everything with religious piety. For example, praying over seed yams and sprinkling them with Holy Water before heading to the farm for planting would seem crazy to a contemporary mind; but that was his practice. I can remember very vividly when we were small, and our big nanny goat gave birth to two kids, Papa gave the kids beautiful names that more or less reflected his piety: he called one Mercy and the other Charity. He gave the two kids to my brother Paul and me. I can't remember now who owned which. We were happy to own goats and we were excited to join other children in the neighborhood who fetched foliage for their goats. Of course, we were just nominal owners; Papa however sold the goats without consulting us, but our joy was in trooping out with other children in the morning to fetch foliage. A lot of things that excited kids in those days are no longer around.

When we were growing up, some villages had a practice of staging intervillage entertainment. One village would visit another to stage a dance. There they performed a traditional dance known as Ekong. The dancers entertained not only with singing and dancing, but the group also ridiculed and presented a caricature of some members of a village they had some dispute with, usually a land dispute. They would ridicule some individuals in the village by impersonating them in a most demeaning manner. These undignified impersonations were what really attracted a lot of people to these shows.

These stage shows included a lot of supernatural displays which people attributed to some devilish power and magic. Of course, that was typical of traditional societies in those days.

Wherever they staged one of these dance shows, everybody in the neighborhood would be there to have fun and enjoy themselves. Whenever the show was staged at "Anwa Ikot Ukpong"(Ikot Ukpong Village Square), we could have gone since it was close to where we lived. Everyone in the neighborhood would go, including children, but Papa would not let us go. He did not want us to be corrupted by the display of magic and charms. He was afraid we might be confused and start to believe in those things. There were many other things like that which we did not get to "enjoy" like other kids, and sometimes we thought that being a catechist's child was not good. But those were just silly childhood moments, for we have grown up to appreciate the fruit of the training he gave us.

There were really very few things that Papa enjoyed. One of them was instructing people. He loved to teach catechism to the people and he spent the greater part of his life doing that. Even when his eyes grew dim and he could not read, still he would teach because the whole text was in his head. At this point he really did not need the books anymore. If the need arose to refer to the Bible, he would cite the text and someone would read for him. Once you were in his presence, you had to be careful in citing the scriptures, for he knew a lot of the text in the Bible. He was a moving biblical concordance.

There were a few days in the life of Papa that were not easy to forget. One of those was the day he personally hosted the bishop of Ikot Ekpene Catholic diocese, His Lordship Bishop Camillus Etokudoh, in our house. When he was on his pastoral visit to Urua Akpan Parish in the Spring of 1999, the bishop specifically made out some time to pay a private visit to Papa in his house—something Papa appreciated as a once-in-a-lifetime honor. It was akin to the Lord's visit to the house of the centurion, who protested because he was not worthy of such a visitor. But in his spirit, the centurion was echoing the words of Elizabeth to the Blessed Virgin Mary. Just as

Elizabeth confessed her unworthiness to host such an august visitor (even though she was her cousin), Papa also found himself unworthy of such a grand visitor; but all the same he felt honored.

Later that day, in a speech made during his reception in the church, the bishop mentioned that he had visited Catechist Obotama that morning because he (Catechist Obotama) was the person who prepared him (Bishop Etokudoh) for Baptism and First Holy Communion. I was in the church that same day, for I was the bishop's secretary then, and I looked at Papa, he gave a very angelic smile; one could perceive the radiating aura of his psyche. He enjoyed such testimonies more than any material wealth.

This incident no doubt provided more material for Papa to use in advising his grandchildren. He always told them to look at the bishop, because "he was very humble as a student and now you see how God has elevated him." Bishop Etokudoh was an idol of some sort for him. Therefore, it was providential that Bishop Etokudoh ordained Rev. Fr. Lawrence Obotama, the last child of the family, in 2007. This was the second priest in Catechist Obotama's family, and although Papa was not physically present to witness the occasion, it is our belief that he was very happy in heaven when his last child was called and ordained on that Saturday, July 28. When I was ordained in that same cathedral 20 years earlier, the commentator at the ordination ceremony, Rev. Fr. John Bosco Ekanem said, "The son is a priest and the father is a catechist." That caused thunderous applause in the cathedral.

Sometimes, in his love for the church, Papa would act in ways that were amusing to us grown-ups in the family. Here is one example. When Papa heard for the first time that Fr. Asuquo Akpan had received a doctorate degree, he was so elated that in his excitement he praised God for blessing our area with a "doctor of the church." I wanted to tell him the difference between a "doctor of the church" and an academic doctor, but I knew he would not believe me, and as long as the news kept him excited I let it go. So Fr. Asuquo Akpan remained for Papa a "doctor of the church." For him, a priest with a doctoral degree is different from a medical doctor. Therefore he is a doctor of the church, not a doctor of medicine. In a way there is some sense in his idea. A priest, no matter how highly educated he may be, still belongs to the church. He is not a doctor for himself only, and therefore Papa's idea seems logical here. He is a "doctor for the church." When I told Papa that Fr. Asuquo Akpan was going to preach at Midim Atan during my second Thanksgiving Mass, which was on July 19, 1987, Papa thought there was no honor greater than that, for a "doctor of the church" to preach at our small station church at Midim.

Papa was always very caring to people, even strangers, but especially religious figures. One day in the early 70s, my little sister Etiido went to our local pond, Aworoto, for water. There she saw a Nun in her white habit coming to fetch water. She was surprised, and came home to tell us the story of how she saw a Nun carrying a bucket of water, which was a rare sight for those of us who were familiar with the Medical Missionaries of Mary Sisters in the hospital. Papa asked her what she did for the Sister. Etiido did not know what to say. Papa ordered her to go back to the pond and fetch water for that Sister whom Papa suspected was a student nurse in the hospital's School of Nursing. Etiido left for water and after about an hour she came back home with the Sister, who identified herself as Sister Regina Eshiet of the Handmaids of the Holy Child Jesus (HHCJ). As Papa had suspected, she was in the School of Nursing. She was so appreciative of what Etiido did that she wanted to come with her to see her parents. Ever since, Sister Regina has been a very good friend of our family. She was of immense help to my family during a very trying period we went through. She was just a God-sent angel to us. That's as much as I can say here, since I do not have her permission to elaborate more; so I will just leave it at that. She was at Papa's funeral at Urua Akpan on July 24, 2002 and again on July 28, 2002, when we had a memorial service for Papa at St. Anthony's Parish Ekpenyong Atai, she was there and spoke so eloquently about Papa.

Papa always believed in the divine origin of marriage—that is, he believed that marriage is of God and therefore every marriage should start with God's blessing. Papa had been a marriage instructor for a long time, and he had witnessed many cases where the parents of the bride posed a problem to the couple who wanted to receive God's blessing in a church wedding. Papa did not want such in our family; he made sure that on the day of the Traditional Marriage of his children, the Parish Catechist must be there to fill out the church marriage forms known as the "marriage banns." That way, the church wedding process was set rolling on the same day that the traditional marriage ceremony took place.

People were surprised in St. Brigid's Catholic community Urua Akpan when Etiido's marriage banns were published for the first time just a day after the traditional marriage. She was the first of our siblings to enter into wedlock. Some people had not even heard of the traditional marriage which took place a day before the publication of the banns. Papa did that again at my brother Paul's traditional marriage, and again with the marriage of my sister Uduak. He personally fixed the church wedding date of Uduak for August 30, 2002, even before the traditional marriage ceremony was held. Unfortunately, he did not get to witness the wedding, as he had to bow to the will of God by answering His call to glory on July 14, 2002.

Papa was not a trained philosopher or theologian, but he often made some philosophical statements that reflected the thinking of some philosophers. He used proverbs, which carry a lot of wisdom in Annang communication system. When Papa noticed that you had failed in following his advice, or that you were not serious about what he wanted you to do, he would always say, "ama item ama ifiok, asua nduari ebiet unam." literally this means he who loves advice loves wisdom but he who hates scolding is an animal. He would always make sure that things were done in the proper way and in the right manner. For him, there was no half way—whatever ought to be done must be done well.

In a normal family setting, parents are often at the mercy of their children. Children can make parents do certain things they would not normally want to do. We children had this effect on Papa, too.

One thing that we never saw Papa did in his lifetime was run. He must have ran when he was young, or probably before we were born; but we never saw him do it—except one time.

One fateful afternoon, I got into a fight with my brother Paul. I can't actually remember very well what brought about the fight—like regular kids, we sometimes got into squabbles. In the fight, Paul hit my wrist with a piece of stick, and when I screamed and started crying, he ran away and Papa ran out and pursued him. Being somewhat small in size, Paul was able to run easily through the market stalls close to our house which usually served as our playground. Papa had to maneuver through them. Paul ran almost to the periphery of Ikot Ukpong on the outskirts of the market before Papa caught up with him. Needless to say, he got the beating of his life.

Since that day, I can't remember of any other time I saw Papa run. Maybe he did it while I was away from home, but I doubt it very much. I do not think any of my siblings saw him run, either. He was blessed with many grandchildren, and those were the ones who would have forced him to run; but it was not so.

I remember a story I was told about Jerome, my brother Marcus' second son, who went to invite Papa to come and play soccer with him. Papa told him to go and call his dad, but Jerome replied that his dad had gone to Ikot Ekpene. He insisted that Papa should come outside and play with him even though the old man was very weak at that time. I do not know how that issue was resolved, but I don't think Papa oblidged him.

Many of Papa's proverbs ring in my brain now. He would tell us in Efik language, "sop ndikop edi kusop nditing"—"Be quick to hear, be slow to speak." He always warned us against saying something we were not sure about. Even if you are sure, he advised, if it does not concern you directly do not be the first to say it unless you are required to comment out of necessity. Only say something when you are sure you can defend what you say. This is a very important advice.

There is one more point in this chapter that I wish to make. In our culture, at least in the Annang culture that I'm a little bit familiar with, when we were growing up, parents did not express their love for their children with outward affection like parents do in the western culture. That does not mean that Annang parents loved their children less. It was very rare to hear a father tell his son, "I love you," like fathers in the western culture do. Rather, you could see a father's affection in his actions, particularly in the way he cared for his children. Some of them were ready to sell their lands in order to keep their kids in schools. The invasion of western culture into our lives has, however, brought about the outward expression of affection like kissing their kids. Parents now say "I love you" to their kids and vice versa.

Papa showed us love in the way he fulfilled his responsibilities to us as a father. He made sure we had all the books we needed at the beginning of a semester, even if it meant spending his last money. I can see this now as a sign of love more than obligation, but we did not fully understand that at that time. We just took it for granted.

There is no doubt that Papa really planted a good seed in the family he raised. We are blessed to have had him as our father. The blessing is more spiritual than material. At the deaconate ordination of my kid brother, Lawrence Obotama, the live-commentator at the occasion, Rev. Fr. Justin Udofia, took time to mention that "one of those ordained today is a brother to Fr. Raphael Obotama, his sister is a Nun, Sr. Maria Obotama and his other brother Paul Obotama is the Parish Chairman of this new Parish inaugurated today—that was the day Immaculate Conception Parish, Ikot Ekpene was inaugurated—We thank God for Catechist Obotama in the way he brought up his family." There was a thunderous applause in the church at Immaculate Conception Parish, Ikot Ekpene. For me, it is not the applause that mattered but the joy of a family that is barely known in the social circles but has been able to produce workers in the Lord's ministry. Right now my sister, Sr. Maria Obotama MMM is the Novice Mistress of their congregation. She has been entrusted with the job of forming potential members of their congregation. This goes back to a family upbringing which is always the basic foundation in the life of any Clergy or Religious. The training in later life only builds on that prime foundation.

7

Our Family Patron Saint

The psalmist says that unless the Lord builds the house, those who build it labor in vain. This is meant to show that God should be the foundation of every family. Every family is like a garden in which seeds are planted. Whatever fruits come forth are the direct result of the labor of the owner of the garden. Having and maintaining a family does not so much depend on wealth. God must always be given a place in the family. This is exemplified in the familiar saying, "a family that prays together stays together." The fruits from such families are always very good fruits.

There are a number of reasons why I always feel blessed to belong in the family of Catechist Mark Obotama and Mma Margaret Obotama. Sometimes I ask myself, if I had been born into some other family, would I have been where I am today? Would I have been a priest, or even a Catholic? Only God knows the best answers to these questions. There are so many things I have learned from my family that I do not think I could have learned from books. One of these is devotion to the Saints.

Since I became an adult, I have had contact with so many families because of my vocation. But there are very few families in my part of the Christian world that have a personal family patron Saint. This refers to a saint that a family has personal devotion to, in much the same way as some families have a family physician or lawyer. We have such a saint in our family: St. John Bosco. I do not know why Papa chose this saint as the patron saint of our family; he did not tell us, and I did not ask him. But when I did a research on the life of this saint, I discovered that there are three things Papa had in common with St. John Bosco. (1)

John Bosco lost his father at the age of two; Papa also lost his father at a very young age. (2) John Bosco did odd jobs to maintain the family; Papa also had to care of himself by doing odd jobs that no child of his age would normally do. (3) John Bosco was interested in teaching young people catechism, and of course Papa started at a very young age teaching catechism in the church, and also served as a station teacher. These similarities may have been what attracted Papa to this particular saint; but on the other hand, Papa may not have known about these similarities at all. Perhaps the White Fathers, who knew St. John Bosco's history very well, introduced Papa to this Saint. Maybe Papa fell in love with the saint after learning about these life similarities, or maybe he adopted St. John Bosco as the family's patron saint out of love for him. It was most likely the latter.

In the years before the Nigeria/Biafra civil war, Papa subscribed to and had been receiving beautiful calendars from the Salesian Society founded by St. John Bosco. He also received some Novena booklets from this group, and he would use these booklets when he prayed. We were too young at that time to read all those booklets; the thing we enjoyed was admiring those colorful pictures on the pages of the Novena booklets and the calendar. I think Papa had a small statue of St. John Bosco; I'm not too sure. Papa would always read the prayers in English after our family prayers, and then would conclude with "Akam Esop Ubon Mme Christian"—"Act of consecration to the college of the Sacred Heart." After the war, Papa did not have contact with the Salesian Society anymore, but that does not mean we forgot about the saint.

I think the biggest problem Papa encountered after the war was foreign currency exchange. In the years before the war, the White Fathers used to help him process the foreign exchange. How they did it I don't know, but I do know that Papa used to pay the subscription regularly and before the end of the year, the Salesian Society would send him a package containing a calendar for the coming year and some religious articles.

So we grew up with this devotion to St. John Bosco. It was therefore a happy coincidence that Fr. John Bosco Ekanem preached at the Thanksgiving Mass we, Fr. Ephraim Umoren and I celebrated at St. Bridget's Parish Church Urua Akpan after our ordination. The family has a lot more devotions now, like the Sacred Heart of Jesus and the Divine Mercy.

While I'm not sure that any of us is still doing that Novena anymore, St. John Bosco remains the patron saint of the family. May be we should restart that Novena now that we can very readily lay hands on them, thanks to the internet. That would help get the younger generation of family members in the family culture. How I wish many families had this practice of devoting themselves to the saints.

8

A Man of Prayer

If a person wishes to remain in touch with God always, prayer is the best way. Prayer keeps one spiritually alive and active. The apostles recognized the power of prayer when they asked the Lord, "Teach us to pray." Luke 11: 1. The Lord promptly granted their request by teaching them the prayer that is famously known as the Lord's Prayer. He even encouraged them to pray unceasingly. Prayer is the line that links us mortals to the creator. God is a Spirit, and the only thing that links us to Him is prayer. It's a communication line that remains open every moment of one's life in this mortal world. Through prayers, the faithful have the protection of God through the angels. He who prays always feels the protection of God in his life. As Pope Benedict XVI puts it, "The person of prayer has the feeling that he lies on a beach, miraculously saved from the pounding of the waves. Human life is surrounded by the snares of evil lying in wait that not only attack the person's life but also aim at destroying all human values. However, the Lord rises to preserve the just and save him."[3]

Papa discovered this truth about prayer very early in his life, and applied it throughout his mortal life. He passed this on to his kids and grandkids. A family legacy has been established—a life of prayer. More often than not, you would find Papa praying, and his prayer time would capture his complete attention. For him, prayer is the most important activity in human life, because it involved communication with the divine which engages the body and the mind. One thing we kids would not dream of doing in Papa's presence was not being serious (or at least looking serious) during prayers. If you slept during prayers

---

[3]   Pope Benedict XVI, An Invitation to Faith, pg60.

you were in for it. I can't remember how many times as a kid my eyelids were pinched for sleeping during prayers. It was pretty difficult for us kids when Papa tried to control our attention—you can imagine kids' attention spans during prayers. Like most parents at that time, Papa did not understand that a short attention span was part of children's psychology. Of course this is totally understandable given their level of exposure to children's psychology at that time.

Prayer sessions were very serious times in our family. Unless you were sick, nobody was allowed to be absent from the family prayers, morning or night. In some cases, Papa would even invite the sick individual to join the family prayers, but allowed him or her the comfort of sitting down instead of kneeling throughout the duration of the prayers. We had to kneel straight up, not leaning on anything. I can still remember how he used to show us pictures of some of the saints in prayer from the Novena booklets, and he told us that when a saint prays, even if he is pinched with a needle he would not notice because his whole attention is focused on God.

Early in the morning, Papa would ring the little chapel bell and everybody would go to the chapel for prayers. Some three days after Papa's funeral, one of our neighbors apparently missed the sound of the bell and came to ask Mama if we were going to do away with the early Morning Prayer because "Ette Mark" had died. I had not gone back to Detroit yet, but I was not at home when he came in and asked this question. When I came back I was told about it, and at first I wanted to be upset; but on the other hand, I thought that just maybe Papa was able to influence our neighborhood by that early morning bell which I did not even know they could hear. If that was so, then it was a credit to Papa. So this exercise of Morning Prayer would continue even in the absence of Papa.

Therefore, I was so encouraged when I arrived home for the ordination and installation of our new bishop, Bishop Camillus Umoh, in October of 2010 and immediately upon my arrival, Fr. Lawrence my brother, who came to Port Harcourt to pick me up at the airport, said, "Father, let's go to the Chapel." And as I entered the chapel, Mama came and tinkled the little chapel bell and the all children in the house gathered in the chapel and we prayed. We thanked God for granting me travelling mercies and bringing me safely back home. So the tradition continues.

On Sundays after Mass, when we got back to the house, Papa would sit us down and asked what was said in church. We had to remember at least one thing that the priest said during the homily. Papa was very strict when it came to our prayer life. Every little child in the family had a rosary and knew how to recite it, because Papa would start teaching us kids how to say the rosary as soon as we could talk. We took turns leading in the rosary during our family prayers. Saying the rosary became such a part of his life that it was just like food for the body; he could not do without the rosary. I must say frankly here that it was not fun for us kids at that time. Even when we came back from the farm during farming season, we expected Papa to understand that we were all exhausted from the hard day's work, and hoped that he would allow us to go to bed after just a few short prayers. But he would still go on with a whole decade of the rosary. If any of us happened to sleep during this time, then he could be sure of getting his eyelid tweaked. Of course, by the time the rosary was concluded all of us would have suffered that fate.

The rosary had become such a part of his life that any time he had nothing to do, he would be saying the rosary. We used to joke that he would rather starve from food than miss saying the rosary. I never saw him spending his leisure time listening to the radio unless there was something very important going on, like when there was a coup in Nigeria and when the Pope came to Nigeria and the ceremony was carried live on the radio. Otherwise he was always in the family chapel praying.

Two days after we (two Nuns, Srs. Mildred Udoh, Imelda Effiong and me) arrived in the United States of America in August of 1999, Fr. Thomas Ebong and Sr. Angela Akpabio, who had been in Detroit for some years, took the three of us sightseeing around the city. We went to Belle Isle and stood on the shore of the river that divides the United States and Canada. While we were walking by the shore, we saw a man and a child, presumably a grandpa and his grandchild. They were fishing in the river. I told them jokingly that if it were my dad, he would be saying the rosary with his grandchild.

It so happened that in October of that same year, Fr. Tom travelled home and I gave him some letters for my parents and siblings. When he went to our home to deliver the letters, my dad was in our family chapel praying the rosary with one of my nephews.

Fr. Tom could not help laughing, and he told them the joke I had made about my dad and the rosary.

Papa was also very good in the use of sacramentals. If there was one sacramental that Papa was liberal in using it was the Holy Water. Anything coming into our house from outside was sprinkled with Holy Water, especially if it came from an unfamiliar place or person. Holy Water was (and still is) never in short supply in our home.

Papa's influence on his grandchildren was equally eloquent. I remember one occasion in 1993 when I was at Ikot Atasung Parish as the Parish Priest. That was the year Rev. Fr. Victor Nyoro CM was ordained. The parish had slaughtered a cow, and out of their appreciation for my work with them and respect for my family, they gave me a huge portion of the meat for my parents. I took the meat home that afternoon. My nephew Emmanuel, whom we call Keresifon, was probably four or five years old then and was living with my parents. As soon as I presented the gift to my parents and said it came from my parish, Emmanuel rushed into the family chapel and brought out the Holy Water and started sprinkling the meat. Mama told me that Papa had instructed him that anything given to him by a stranger should be sprinkled with Holy Water before using it. By the way, Keresifon (Emmanuel) is a fourth-year philosophy student at St. Joseph's Major Seminary—Ikot Ekpene as I am writing this book now.

Papa's devotion to the Eucharist was remarkable. For him, the Holy Mass was his life. He would always go to the church to visit the Blessed Sacrament. He never missed Mass unless he was extremely sick. I had never seen any day that Papa missed communion at Mass, unless he was attending a second or third Mass as he would do any time he had the opportunity. He actually believed that his spiritual strength came from the Eucharist. Therefore he made it an obligation to receive communion daily. He also wanted us kids to receive communion daily and in the proper decorum.

One morning we came back from church, and he called me and asked me a catechism question which had to do with the reference after the reception of the Holy Communion. I answered correctly, and then he asked me, "Did you do that today at Mass after communion?" The answer was no; in this case, I had been distracted by one of our cousins who used to live with us. Her name was Eno, and she was there at Mass that day. I got away with just a scolding from Papa.

Looking at Papa's devotion to the Eucharist, one cannot fail to see a reflection of the words of Blessed John Paul II: "From the Eucharist comes strength to live the Christian life and zeal to share that life with others." Papa was truly a model to many people.

One signature prayer that Papa often used was from the book of psalms: "O Obong yak Ima Afo odoro nnyin k'idem kpa nte nnyin idoride fi enyin"—"May your love be upon us O Lord as we place all our hope in you." (Ps.32) He concluded every family prayer session with those words, placing his hands on his chest and bowing in obeisance. We all joined. Even right now as I'm writing I can still visualize him in that position in my mind. It became a family practice, and very providentially that was the response to the responsorial psalm at the Mass of my ordination on May 17, 1987 in St. Anne's Cathedral—Ifuho, Ikot Ekpene. As I watched the playback of the video recording of the ordination ceremony some days later, it really gave me food for thought watching and listening to the choir sang that response. I don't even think Papa or any other member of the family had observed that as the ceremony was going on, because everybody was anxious to see the ordination rite. In my personal reflection I thought, God really loves our family. So the prayers we had been offering in the family had not escaped the notice of God. How else could one explain such a wonderful coincidence on such a very a special day in the life of our family? At the ordination of a member of the family to the priesthood, a psalm that had become a signature of the family for many decades was chosen as a responsorial psalm for the ordination Mass without even our asking.

Papa was very good in the recitation of psalms. There were only a few psalms in the Bible that Papa did not know by heart. He taught us some of the psalms, but many of them we just picked them up as we prayed daily.

What keeps a family united and secured is not material wealth bequeathed to them by parents, but the good legacy parents leave behind for their children—especially when this legacy is spiritual. Papa instilled in us faith in God and obedience to the authorities of the Church—characteristics he had in abundance. A combination of these traits has become our family culture. We are blessed that he left this religious legacy for our family which is more valuable than wealth, because in some cases wealth turns out to be a problem for the children and often splits a family.

Our spiritual lives were paramount to Papa. Even as kids he would lead us every Saturday evening to the church for confession in preparation for the Sunday Mass. Sometimes we thought we did not have anything to confess, and so we had to confess even things that were not necessary. That may not have been the best way of training kids, but that was what he knew, and I can say that it served a good purpose. It turned out well for him and us.

We have tried to maintain one particularly eloquent tradition that Papa started—the end-of-year family Mass. On the last day of every year, December 31, the whole Nto Akpan Nna family would gather together for a Thanksgiving Mass. I cannot remember the exact year he started it, but I do remember that I was in the Junior Seminary at Afaha Obong. When we first started this tradition, we used to go to our family home at Ikot Inyang Udo for the Mass. Papa would write out the names of all the departed members of the family and place the list on the altar. He included everybody, whether baptized or not. I remember writing the names out in cursive handwriting on a cardboard paper and framing it. We stopped using the list when there were some recent deaths in the family that a new list was required. At that point then, Papa would simply mention the intention at the beginning of the family Mass. Before my ordination, he used to invite the parish priest to come and celebrate the Mass. After my ordination in 1987, I would leave whichever parish I was and went home to celebrate the end-of-year Mass. I did this until when I left for studies in 1999. For a few years thereafter, another priest was invited to come and celebrate the Mass until my brother Fr. Lawrence Obotama was ordained in 2007.

Papa was poor materially, but very rich spiritually, and we can see the result of his riches in the strong faith of his family. He made sure that he bequeathed that heritage to his children. Up until he entered into eternal life, he always believed that he had a spiritual obligation towards his kids and even his grandkids. He always wanted to know if each of us had fulfilled our spiritual obligations, such as those at Easter. Even some of my grown up siblings with families were still under his watchful eyes before he passed. He always monitored how they were doing with their families spiritually.

Another family tradition we learned from Papa is the end-of-year ritual. At the stroke of midnight on the last day of the old year rolling into the first day of the New Year, he would go outside to remove the Christmas decorations of palm fronds and flowers that we had excitedly fixed on Christmas Eve. But first he would offer some private prayers and then remove the decorations according to our local practice. When he came back to the house he would wake all of us up for a family prayer which would last no less than 30 minutes. During this time we would be distracted by people shouting and running around as they "chased away" the old year and ushered in the New Year. People would be firing guns in the air, firing home-made fireworks and throwing the whole area into a celebratory frenzy as the New Year rolled in. I do not know how much we as little kids really concentrated during the prayers with such pandemonium going on outside on the streets. However, those midnight New Year's prayers have become a lovely tradition which I am happy to continue. When I was in the parish, I made certain to usher in the New Year with the celebration Mass with the people. Even when I was a student and not serving in any parish, I made it my duty to celebrate Mass starting at 11:45pm, so that the New Year meets me on the altar of sacrifice. I enjoy it and I keep doing it.

Papa was so prayerful that the church, which is just a short walking distance from our house, literally became his home after his retirement. He spent more time in the church than in the house until his health started failing him. A onetime parish priest was quoted as saying that given a chance, he would recommend Catechist Obotama for ordination. In Nigeria we do not have permanent diaconate program as in the United States.

When his eyes grew dim, Papa would ask my brother Nnabuk, now Fr. Lawrence, who was then in the seminary to come at about 7pm to lead him back from the church, because he could no longer see very well at night. When Lawrence was back in the seminary, Marcus would do it.

Papa was an avid reader of the Bible, and he knew almost every story in the Bible. He could tell when someone made a mistake in citation. He could tell all the stories in the Bible. He was a living concordance.

He could refer you to any area in the Bible that dealt with any particular theme you asked him about.

Papa embraced the devotion to the Sacred Heart after the Nigeria/Biafra war. Before the war I did not hear of this devotion; our family prayed to St. John Bosco. I was amused one day in my primary school years when we were at Okon Parish. I came back from school one day and saw a little handbook of the Sacred Heart of Jesus on his reading table. What amused me was the name written on it: "PROMOTER OBOTAMA." When I saw this I chortled, thinking in my childish imagination that Papa had taken a nickname, because I knew a guy who was called "Show Promoter" as a nickname. Later that year, I came to know that "Promoter" is just a title in the Sacred Heart League.

Papa introduced this devotion into our family and he never missed the First Friday Devotion, which we all had to attend. What we kids hated about it was that we had to fast from morning until after the devotion at noon or there about. That was not very popular with us kids. What saved us was school—we could not participate when the school was in session. But when school was out for vacation, we had to be there in the church until noon. This devotion to the Sacred Heart became part of our family culture as early as 1970. It is not surprising that my mom and my brother Marcus are still Promoters of the Sacred Heart League while Fr. Lawrence Obotama is the diocesan Chaplain of the Sacred Heart League in Ikot Ekpene. Even now that is one of the major devotions of our family.

Papa was a member of the Pioneer Total Abstinence Association when we were growing up. He recruited us into the association even as kids. We were forbidden from drinking alcoholic beverages. When we kids would visit with some of our playmates, and their parents offered us the local palm wine, we could not drink it. We would always tell them we were "Pioneers." Did we really understand what we were doing ? that I do not know. The first time I ever tasted our local palm wine was in 1970 when we were at Okon Parish. Papa had been advised by the doctor to drink it, because he said it was rich in yeast which was good for the eyes. Papa did not want to heed to the advice of the doctor, so he reported it the parish priest, Fr. Obot, who asked him not to ignore the doctor's instructions. It was then that we all started drinking palm wine and all other alcoholic beverages.

Papa had utmost respect for sacred spaces. He taught us to respect them as well. He expected us to display the proper comportment when in a scared space, especially where the Blessed Sacrament was present. He would always tell us that this is the house of God. He taught us to observe the little light in the sanctuary—the tabernacle light. Any time we entered a church and the light was on, we should know that the Blessed Sacrament was there, and that Jesus was present in the tabernacle (sanctuary). We could not imagine talking or laughing in a church, or doing anything that could be considered irreverent—especially when the Blessed Sacrament was present. Any such misbehavior would earn us severe beatings. Even the little family chapel at home was considered a scared space, and as such should be given due respect. Children were not allowed to go in there in their flip-flops (slippers). Every child in the family knew the rules of utter respect for sacred spaces. You do not misbehave in the church and get away free, unless you were fortunate not to be caught by Papa or someone who could report you to him.

I can still remember the beating I had one evening when I was a kid, because I laughed in the church during benediction. I have forgotten what caused me to laugh, but I was unfortunate to be caught by Papa. When we arrived home he asked me why I laughed in the church, and I could not answer; no excuse would have been good enough to justify my laughing in the church. So I kept rather quiet and got what I deserved. I would not like to relive that moment.

Papa's legacy remains evergreen in the family. I was so excited when I called my brother Fr. Lawrence one day, and he told me how he was celebrating Masses in the outstations of his parish. Then he added, "Do you remember what Papa used to say about celebration of Masses to the people?" He told me how he was doing the visitation. He would start with Confession, Mass, and then the exposition of the Blessed Sacrament; and while the people were adoring the Blessed Sacrament, he visited the sick in the station to give them communion. I was happy that he could still remember what Papa used to say about being pastorally-minded as a priest. My joy is that Papa's legacy will ever continue. Fr. Lawrence was just a seminarian when Papa passed, yet he still remembered those things Papa said, and still practiced them. I'm sure Papa would be happy to see that we are keeping to his words.

Let me conclude this chapter in a funny way. There is one song that will always remind me of Papa. Every time we had Mass at home, even when I was not yet ordained, at offertory he would always sing "Ini Ekem yak nkewa uwa ekom, yak nkewa uwa ekom, yak nkewa uwa ekom nno Abasi"—"It's time for me to offer a sacrifice of thanksgiving to God." I always remember him getting up and leading the family in procession to put the offerings in the tray. He was always in his best mood when he attended Mass.

9

A Man Committed to Work

I am very sure Papa did not read any of the writings of St. Augustine, but he surely lived according to the admonition of this saint who advised, "Pray as if everything depended on God. Work as if everything depended on you." I can summarize Papa's life this way: If prayers took first place in Papa's life, then work certainly took a very close second. In contemporary vocabulary, he would be described as a workaholic. He had a reputation for being completely committed to whatever he set his mind to do, including responsibilities he was given by someone else.

Papa did not tolerate idleness. If you were the kind of guy who would always take your time and do your work at your own leisure, chances are that you and Papa would not have been the best of pals. He believed very strongly in working hard to earn one's own living. If he saw you idle, he would always find something for you to do. That was one of the reasons that we abhorred staying with him at the station; but there was nothing we could do. We were kids, so we had to go with him as long as we were in school. The only way we escaped him was to be busy doing nothing whenever he was around. We wanted to be free to play, so we would pretend to be doing something until he left. If he was going out, such as going to Ifuho for diocesan meeting, he would always assign some work to us before leaving that would keep us busy until he came back. So we would just hide away until he left.

He liked to quote the famous adage that an idle mind is the devil's workshop. To keep us from becoming the devil's workshop, he would always engage us in some activities, and sometimes he would ask us to go get our books and come sit in the same room with him and read while he was doing something else.

The circumstances of Papa's birth and early childhood caused him to hold strongly to one philosophy—if you must have anything, you must have to work for it. The days of manna falling in the desert were long gone; you must work for what you need. He did not believe in looking up to someone else to give him his heart's desire. Growing up as an orphan in extreme poverty, he would not stretch his hands where he knew he might not reach. He would not beg anybody for anything, for according to him, if you beg for something and the person denies you that thing, then you are defeated. Always work for what you want. Whatever you work for will always be your own. For him, that was the only way to succeed in life. He did not believe in thrusting his needs in some other person's hands. If help happened to come his way from somebody, he would of course appreciate it. Papa warned us to steer clear of certain practices you see in today's society, such as expecting to receive but being unwilling to work. He always told us that the devil sets a trap for those who want to gain more than they work for. He would repeat that always as if we had not heard it before.

As I mentioned, he was very good in proverbs like any orthodox Annang person. There was one proverb we always used, which he repeated so many times that we knew it as his signature. Whenever he heard us laughing and having fun when there was some work to be done, he would come around and say, "What are you doing whiling away this time when there is something out there to be done?" And he would say, "nduok odudu ofon k'utom amakure"—"business before pleasure." Those were his famous sayings. When he was out of sight, we would laugh and ask whenever that time would come—of course, that was in our teen years.

Whenever he had something serious to say, he would unconsciously mix both Efik language and Annang dialect, and when he did that, we knew he was very serious and if you happen to be the reference point you know you are in for a problem. It was only when we were grown up that we used to laugh about it with him and he would simply laugh, but we would not dream of ever doing that many years back when we were still very young and he was still very energetic.

These things led to Papa inculcating in all of us the spirit of dedication to duty. He taught us that once we were assigned something to do, we must see it as a responsibility that must be carried out. This philosophy can sometimes be a weakness, because you can totally lose yourself in your endeavor to fulfill an assignment. Sometimes, even in the midst of sickness, I still feel I have to do what I'm supposed to do as a matter of obligation.

I believe that if everybody were to see life through the same prism as Papa, a lot of things would change in the world today. We live in a society where people only believe in quick gains without labor, and the results here is chaotic. This is why there are crimes today—people just want to reap where they did not sow or reap a lot where they sowed a little.

10

A Simple, Respectful, and Peaceful Person

His early life influenced Papa a great deal. It formulated his personal philosophy, which he made sure to transfer to his family. He had his idea of the type of family he wanted to raise.

One thing that never ceased to amaze me about Papa was his level of contentment. He was always satisfied with the little he had in his life. He was not demanding, and always appreciated any little thing he was given. He never clamored for what others had so that he could be in line with others. He was satisfied with just being himself, even after my ordination, he never once asked me to come and solve any family financial problems. Instead, he would struggle and find a solution himself.

Once a "concerned friend" came up to Papa and inquired why I did not build a house for the family as other priests were doing. This friend suggested that Papa should ask me to come and take up another job so that I could help the family more. To the friend's utter embarrassment, Papa said to him that "Father did not go into the priesthood so as to help the family." He told the friend that he was satisfied with being poor rather than asking his son to stretch his hands beyond his reach, just to build a house for the family or take care of some family responsibilities. The "concerned friend" was totally embarrassed and walked away from the house. I just heard about that encounter a few years ago, a long time after Papa had passed on, from one of my siblings. The shocking thing about the incident is that the "concerned friend" was supposed to know more about the priesthood than Papa.

When I was in seminary, I overheard Papa and some other catechists discussing several issues about the Church. I was in my room and they were in the living room, but I could hear everything they were saying. What actually was interesting was their concept of the priesthood. For Papa, the priesthood was a vocation, not a profession. One did not go into the priesthood to be rich. Once a man became a priest, the whole church became his family, which is why he was called Father by all. Surprisingly, Papa never had this type of discussion with me about the priesthood. He had the deepest respect for the priests.

Papa was a simple, humble, but very firm person. He was respectful. His simplicity was not a mark of low self-esteem. He always stood for what was right; he was not afraid to speak his mind if he needed to, no matter whose ox got gored. In my entire life I can only remember two occasions when he shouted at another fellow, and only once had I heard of him being in a physical struggle with another man.

He was in a physical confrontation with a Biafran soldier once when we were kids. I can still remember a case during the civil war, when we fled Urua Akpan and camped at Ikot Akpan Eka. My parents visited home regularly to fetch some needed items, sometimes twice a day. Urua Akpan at that time was occupied by the Biafran soldiers. One evening Papa came to the house, and as he opened the front door he could hear some pounding sound from inside the house. He followed the sound and came face to face with a soldier breaking down the window of the bedroom from the backyard. He questioned him, and the soldier responded that he just came in to inspect the place which he noticed had been broken into. Papa pointed out that he (Papa) had been there that morning and nothing had happened to the house; and as Papa was saying this, the soldier tried to run away but Papa grabbed him. A struggle ensued, at which point the soldier slipped off his jacket and ran away. Unfortunately for him, his ID was in the pocket of his jacket; fortunately for Papa, there were some soldiers who mounted a check point down the street before the parish house, and they knew Papa very well, because Papa used to give them some of the freshly-tapped wine whenever it was available. He ran to them with the jacket and reported the case, and they followed him to the house. They were able to identify the soldier, and confirmed that they had heard the pounding but did not pay much attention to it, thinking that it was probably Papa doing some repair work. They were still inspecting the place when the soldier came back with more soldiers with him. Apparently, he had lied to the Commanding Officer that some civilians were trying to kill him. But the group of soldiers with Papa told the truth, and when the other soldiers found out what really happened, they turned against the soldier who had tried to break in. They took him away, this time as a culprit. Whatever happened to him after that we did not know. That night we prayed for him during our family prayers.

Papa was extraordinarily simple and very obedient to authority, especially church authority. When I was in the Junior Seminary at Afaha Obong, a one-time rector scolded papa in the presence of many students without regards for human dignity and no respect for human feelings. It had to do with school fees, and he spoke to my dad in so demeaning a tone that if I'd had the guts, I would have voluntarily left the seminary that day. I was so embarrassed that I cried, but my father did not seem to be offended at all. Rather, he apologized to the rector even though this was very clearly not Papa's fault at all, but an administrative miscalculation. He simply wanted clarification on some issues. Although none of this was his fault, in Nigeria, the person in authority is always right.

It saddened me that authority figures could not humble themselves and admit their mistakes. They would not accommodate those who are considered as commoners. That day I made a private promise to God that if I became a priest, I would not disrespect any person. I have tried to live up to that, and I pray that God will always give me the grace to regard every human being as a creature of God who deserves respect.

Even today, I still remember this incident. That's the thing about hurting a person who is very young and has no way of retaliating. It is difficult for young children to forget such things. But Papa did not harbor any ill feelings toward the rector. He simply advised me to behave.

There was another incident where Papa exhibited great respect for a religious authority. In my home diocese, the summer holidays is usually a time that seminarians on vacation tour the stations and conduct retreat. The Parish Priest or the Catechist would draw up a schedule for this exercise. Each station was to come to pick up the seminarians at the parish center on the scheduled day and drop them off at the end of the exercise. But one station failed to come for their seminarian, and the parish priest blamed it on

Papa. The priest said that he (Papa) did not inform the station. Papa told him that all the stations were informed, and other stations had come for their seminarians. The priest decided to go by himself and drop off the seminarians in the station. Unfortunately, he had a flat tire on the way, and when he returned he withheld Papa's salary for two months to pay for the tire. The parish council unanimously decided that the case should be reported to the Cardinal, but Papa persuaded them not to. He decided to "carry that cross," even though there were four of us in school at the time. This story was retold at Papa's funeral Mass by the homilist who was one of the seminarians in the car that night.

Papa was the most peaceful person I have ever known. He went about his work quietly and did not have any problems with anybody. In the whole neighborhood there is not a single soul who could accuse Papa of having had any problem with him or her. We are proud of the kind of life he lived, and we count ourselves blessed to have had him as our father.

Having a catechist for a father imposed special responsibilities on us as we were to be shining examples to other kids in our neighborhood. Any act of disobedience or disrespect to an elder was met with punishment. I remember one time when I talked back disrespectfully at a neighbor. His name was Dan, but the women and young adults used to call him Ette Dan. When Papa found out that I had spoken disrespectfully to Ette Dan, I received a serious beating that left scars not just on my body—it left a deep mark on my psyche. Papa threatened to stop me from ever going to the sacristy again, thereby cutting me off from the altar service which he knew I really loved. I think he had the impression that I learned the "bad habit" of talking back (even though I did it only once) from my peers in the school and in the sacristy. Mama's intervention and my subsequent promise never to ever talk back at any senior person changed Papa's mind, and he allowed me to go back to the sacristy.

Every one of us in the family can tell one story or another like this one. We all had similar experiences with Papa's discipline while we were growing up. There is one exception in the family, and that is our last brother, Nnabuk—Fr. Lawrence. He grew up when Papa did not have that vibrancy in him anymore; he didn't have the energy to run after Nnabuk like he used to do with us when we were

124

growing up. Fr. Lawrence happens to be the most independent-minded one in the family, and he is the only one who is unafraid to speak his mind, although he does it with great respect. The rest of us grew up being cowed into obsessive obedience to the point that we all grow up to be introverts. This sometimes makes it difficult to speak our mind, even when our rights are being trampled upon. We were raised like many other kids in our time; it was thought that that was the only way to train kids—to make them be seen and not heard. The children's job was simply to listen and take orders.

Sometimes, our parents thought that by being so strict they would be able to train their children to be good kids. To have kids who were disrespectful was seen as a failure on the part of the parents—disrespectful children were a clear sign of irresponsibility on the part of the parents. Respectful children, on the other hand, were a glory to the parents. That was the responsibility imposed on the parents by societal expectation and cultural norms. Thank God a lot of that has changed now. In our own case, Papa went the extra mile with discipline since he was a catechist.

Teachers were also forced into strict disciplinary actions by societal expectations. Certain areas were off-limits, and we could not go out and play in these unapproved areas like other children. If we happened to sneak out to such forbidden places when Papa was out, we had to be very watchful and dive back to the house immediately upon sighting him from afar. Otherwise, we had to prepare our rear ends for the cane.

In addition to respecting the elders, Papa taught us to respect the law. He told us that every law comes from God, and therefore that law must be observed if we want to go to heaven. Rules and norms were to be respected. Papa held this philosophy as his personal conviction, not just because of societal expectations, even though those also played a part. His personal philosophy actually played a more decisive role in the way we were brought up.

Sometimes I wonder if this was the best way to bring up kids. When they are cowed into obsessive obedience, that even at old age it is difficult to say no to someone. But on the other hand, our upbringing has also saved us from a lot of trouble which we would have otherwise gotten into if we weren't respectful. Papa's respect for even the smallest individual he came in contact with amazed us children. I guess the Bible really influenced his personal life. His world view was always through the lens of the scripture and the teachings of the church. It could be said that he was fanatical about his faith, but without being aggressive toward those who were not of his faith. He respected other people's opinions without compromising his own belief. I could see this very well when I was a kid—I saw how he argued with the Jehovah's Witness members who came to our house occasionally to preach. He would gently put across his argument with copious citations from the Bible without being disrespectful. Everything he said he would back it up with the scripture, lending credence to his statement.

11

The Lighter Side of Him

From what you have read so far about Catechist Obotama, you may picture a man as quiet and as serious as a monk, right? You would be dead wrong.

One side of Papa that was unknown to a lot of people was his lighter side. But anyone who in our house for just a little while would surely experience his sense of humor. Even though he was quiet and reserved, he had time to deliver some rib-cracking jokes. He knew the right time to say something funny. Most of the time he used jokes to diffuse tension, particularly on the farm when he noticed that we were all tired out. Despite how exhausted we were, everyone would end up laughing hysterically.

He also enjoyed good humor when you presented it at the appropriate time. I must have been influenced by Papa's sense of humor, because I find myself dishing out jokes often, mostly when I'm in a friendly environment. People close to me seem to enjoy my sense of humor, but some people misunderstand me and take it as a lack of seriousness. But I have no problem with such folks, because everybody is entitled to his own opinion.

Humor adds a very good flavor to homily presentations. Papa never attended a single class in homiletics, but he had his own style of homily presentation. He would use proverbs (which he loved) and some stories, which helped drive home the message. Despite his lack of training, Papa always preached convincingly, and that's what makes the difference at the end of the day. We will always miss him.

12

∽

And One by One He Named Them

Many of the names that are given show people's religious feelings. This practice is found all over Africa. . . . Therefore it is no wonder that many African names reflect the religious feelings of the parents concerned.

—John Mbiti

In his encounter with a strange being in the burning bush in the book of Exodus, Moses insisted on knowing the name of the person with whom he was speaking. He argued that the people of Israel, whom he was being sent to lead, would only believe him if they knew the identity of the person they were dealing with. A name meant a lot for the people of that time. People may casually ask, "What's in a name?" I truly believe that there is much in a name. Every Annang person knows this. Some of the elaborate naming ceremonies in certain ethnic groups in Nigeria also testify to this belief. I personally am convinced that there is a lot in a name, especially as it relates to my family history.

In almost every culture in Africa, oral tradition is paramount for the preservation of history; most of the stories about a people, events, and places are woven into folk tales, songs and names. In many cultures, names preserve history. A given name in Annang tradition tells more history than most names in western cultures, where some parents choose names that appeal to their fancy for their children. In Annang tradition, a family history may be packed into a name. At other times, the story of a parent is reflected in the name they give to their child. Each child's name has a deep meaning either to the parents or the child (or to both).

As John Mbiti said in the quote above, religious beliefs also play a role in the names given to children. The Annangs are very religious, and the contemporary children's names depict these religious beliefs. They portray the relationship of the parents with the object of their belief. Even in biblical times, names were essential to revealing the relationship between God and His people. Names in every African culture tell stories. If we go by the theory that a name tells a story, and stories are what make history alive, then Papa's history lives on in our family names (although this is not the main focus of this project). Hopefully someone in the family will take up the task of writing the theological reflection of all the names in our family tree.

Almost all of the names of the children and grandchildren in our immediate family reflect Papa's belief and faith. He was someone who put his faith into practice at every point in his life on earth. Thus, another way of assessing Papa's faith would be to look at the names in our family circle.

The names of the three archangels, Raphael, Gabriel, and Michael are reflected in our family names. From the early stage of Papa's life, we have been able to feel the intervening power of these archangels. I used to ask myself why I was named Raphael, given that I was not even born on the feast day of this archangel (a lot of Catholic parents in those days used to name their children according to the feast day on which the child was born). It was not until I was in the Senior Seminary that I found out that Papa had a more theological reason why he called me this Hebrew-originated name, Raphael. When the Medical Missionaries of Mary at Urua Akpan, effected his healing in the early part of his life when he had severe sickness, it was nothing short of the miraculous healing power of God. That is why he named me Raphael—"God has healed"—or as some people translate it, "The healing of God." He saw the hand of God in the miracle of his health, and therefore he named his first child to commemorate this healing experience. So Raphael is therefore invoked not just as the healing angel in Papa's case, but as the healing angel of our whole family.

At the time God delivered Papa, not many people in the village where he came from really knew or believed in the Christian God. He always told us that God took him from among his people as he took Abraham away from his homeland to a foreign land, so that he might become a blessing to the people of his little-known village.

According to this naming custom, Papa named my brother Paul, "Edidiong"—Blessing. Our theocentric names were not very popular, so his baptismal name, Paul, became the primary name for him.

Another very significant name in the family is Uduak. The name in its full potency is UDUAK ABASI—"The Will of God." It portrays the extent to which Papa relied on the will of God, and how he went the extra mile to make sure the will of God was held supreme in the family. He was a man who believed that nothing happens without the will of God. He used to tell us that God knows what is good for us and goes ahead to grant it.

Marcus is named after Papa; the name has the same root as Mark, so he is Papa's namesake—"Kokoette." When Marcus was growing up, "Kokoette" was actually the name he used to call him. When Papa could not read anymore, Marcus was always with him. During instructions and some other prayer sessions in the church, Papa would cite the scripture and Marcus would read it, and then

Papa would give the instruction. It was very easy for someone to mistake Marcus for a "catechist intern." No wonder he is the only one of our siblings who is a Promoter of the Sacred Heart League as Papa was. Mama of course still remains a Promoter.

Maria was fondly named "Idong-Esit"— consolation as I mentioned earlier in this book. In our tradition, any child born immediately after the death of a sibling in the family is seen as a consolation to the family. So since Maria was born after the death of our sister Rose, she became a consolation to the family.

Etiido was born during the Nigerian/Biafran war. In papa's personal philosophy, no good deeds go without blessings. It is always good to be good. During the war there were many refugees living in our house who were displaced by the war, and Papa would go all out to make sure they were comfortable, even to the extent of depriving us of some comfort. He tried to share what he had with the refugees. Sometimes when he harvested some yams he would give them some of the tubers also. Etiido was a name that proclaimed Papa's state of mind during the war. Even after the war, anyone who met Papa could not fail to notice this humane trait in him.

Nnabuk is the baby of the family. He is the summation of all the emotions and endurance that Papa and the whole family had gone through. He is the armor bearer of family history, and he is the griot of the family. He is more of a platform on which stories are told about the family. On the day that Nnabuk (Rev. Fr. Lawrence Obotama) celebrated his second Thanksgiving Mass in our station church at Midim Atan, the village head of Ikot Inyang Udo, Chief Godwin Udotim Idio Udoikpa gave a brief history of the supernatural healing of Papa in his speech at the reception. This confirms the contextual meaning of the name "Nnabuk"—"the living shall tell the goodness of God." As the psalmist says, "I will proclaim and tell of them, yet they are more than can be told . . ." Psalm 40: 5. The story of God's healing power made manifest in Papa shall be told by every living person who witnessed his history. Nnabuk's name therefore summarizes his role. Nnabuk was born at a period Papa would call "the looking back,"—a kind of exodus story. At the Thanksgiving Mass I mentioned earlier the village head of Ikot Inyang Udo gave a snippet of what Papa went through as an infant in his village, and how God led him to safety at Urua Akpan. The name "Nnabuk" does not just refer to Papa telling the story of his life, but by extension it means that whomever is alive will always tell the story of the way God delivered Catechist Obotama.

When the first grandchild of the family was born, his father gave him the name Emmanuel. Isaiah the messianic prophet interpreted this name to mean "God is with us," indeed Obotama's family can always say that God is with us. He was also given a very interesting vernacular name, "Keresifon," meaning "always think right, have pure thoughts." I am convinced that the legacy of Ette-Obot (as we fondly called him) will ever continue. The many blessings of God that he experienced in his life gave him hope for more things in the future. So when Paul's first child came, he personally named him "Idorenyin"—Hope. As I mentioned earlier in this book, he would always say "Obong yak Ima afo Odoro nnyin k'idem kpa nte nnyin idoride fi enyin"—"Let your love be upon us O lord as we place our trust in You." So the name "Idorenyin Paul Obotama" is a personification of that unflinching hope in the God who saves us.

And of course, whoever has such an unflinching hope in God is always full of good news. The first daughter of Marcus was uniquely named "Eti-Mbuk," meaning "Good news." It is our family prayer that we keep on hearing good news as we place all our hope in God. This good practice continues even after Papa has passed on. The power of prayers is portrayed by the name of one of Marcus's other daughter, "Ufon Akam"—"the benefits of prayer."

13

The Setting of the Sun

The book of Ecclesiastes says that there is time for everything under the sun, a time to be born and a time to die. Ecclesiates 3:2. It is a metaphysical necessity that whatever has a beginning must have an end. Human beings also follow this metaphysical law, though sometimes we do not feel comfortable accepting the reality of an end when it finally comes. The sun that rises in the morning brings a new day, and no matter how much we enjoy the daylight the sun must ultimately set, bringing the day to an end.

Human life could be metaphorically described this way: we have a morning, midday, and evening which ushers in the sun set. If one is blessed to pass through these three stages, then one is said to have reached a full age. The book of psalms says, "Their span is seventy years or eighty for those who are strong." Psalm 90:10. Papa was blessed to pass through these stages even though none of them was very smooth, but he made it to the end. We thank God who promised to be his God throughout his life. A Negro spiritual in my vernacular says that each person has two important days in a life time: the day of his birth and the day of his death. What matters is what a person does with all the days in between these two days. Death, as the saying goes, is an inevitable end; each person faces it when his or her time comes. It is simply the law of nature.

Papa retired in 1985 from being a diocesan Catechist. That was my second year in the Theology Seminary. My fear then was that, being the type of person he was, he would develop some sort of sickness because he was too full of zeal for his work to retire. Retirement would be too boring for him, I thought. It was not long before I discovered how wrong I was in engaging in an unnecessary worry.

Of course Papa did not just fold his hands and sit back at home after he retired as a catechist. Rather, he continued to do some skeletal catechetical duties in the Parish Church, Urua Akpan. He spent more time in the church just praying the rosary and doing Stations of the Cross and some private devotions.

Not long after his retirement, his eye problems, which he had been suffering from for some time, developed into glaucoma. He was diagnosed by the doctors at the Mercy Hospital Abak. The eye problem became so serious that he could not read, even with his glasses. Somebody suggested surgery for him, but the optician suggested otherwise, telling him that it would not make any difference. His eye problem did not stop him from instructing the people. As I mentioned before, even when his eyes had grown dim, he would go along to church with Marcus who would read for him, and he continued the instructions. He kept struggling with that, and shortly thereafter he developed hypertension which became so severe that I was afraid he would not live to witness my ordination to the priesthood. God preserved his life and he witnessed not only my ordination, but also the final Profession of my Sister, Sr. Maria, in the Medical Missionaries of Mary congregation. He also witnessed the weddings of three of his children—Etiido, Paul, and Marcus. He was just a couple of months shy of witnessing the wedding of his last daughter, Uduak, when he died.

Papa's life was therefore what could be described as fulfilled and blessed. He was still very active until late 90s. During this period of ill-health, he depended a lot on medication; because he took it faithfully, he could still move about, albeit fragilely. Papa was very devoted to anything he set his mind to do, including medications. He took them very religiously. He would never dream of missing his medication.

The day I left for studies in the fall of 1999, I went home to greet him and knelt down before him and asked for his prayers. He prayed for me and asked God to protect me on the journey and keep me safe and finally bring me back. I gave him a hug and then drove out. That was my last meeting with him physically on this earth. At the start of the new millennium, he became physically weak, and most of the time he would remain in our private chapel praying the rosary. He had to be taken to see his cardiologist at Uyo for check-ups because the hypertension had become uncontrollable. I was getting updates on his health here in the States through letters from my brother Paul. At that time, the cell phone companies did make their in-roads into the Nigerian space; so to get information from home, we wrote letters. It was not easy—I had to wait for two to three weeks before getting any update on the state of his health. If anyone was traveling to Nigeria, I did not fail to utilize the opportunity, and I asked that person to help me deliver those letters at home and report back when he or she returned.

One of the parishioners in Detroit gave me a large package containing many rosaries. I sent them all to Papa. From the reports I got, those rosaries were the best thing I ever gave him in his entire life. He was giving them out to friends who visited him in the house. Once I sent him some pictures of the Divine Mercy, and he showed them to the parish priest, who at that time was Monsignor Francis Iyire. Papa had a lot of encouragement from him to start the devotion there in the parish. So he did, and had a very encouraging response from the people. I think the devotion is still being carried on there now.

I can say with certainty that Papa's earthly life was particularly mapped out by the divine creator. I witnessed many events in his life which led me to believe this. Two weeks before he passed away, I was fortunate to speak with him from Detroit. By this time in 2002, the Medical Missionaries of Mary Sisters at Urua Akpan had installed a phone line in the convent. It was a land line. When I was given the phone number, I spoke with the Sisters a couple of times, and then asked them to get my parents to come to the convent so I could speak with them. On the day I was to speak with them, due to the time difference (their morning being our midnight), I spent the whole night trying to get through to Urua Akpan but could not. As God would have it, after trying the line for about eight hours, I was able to get through. By this time, they had left and gone back home, so one of the maids in the convent had to rush to our home to bring them back while I was hanging on the phone waiting for them. It was time well-spent—I did not care how much it would cost me; I was determined to speak with them. They arrived, and I was able to speak with them a little, I did not know that it would be my last conversation with Papa in this earthly life.

The Medical Missionary Sisters who were the reason he moved into Urua Akpan in the first place, were the same Religious Sisters who helped me connect with him before he passed. They will always remain a part of our family history, not just because my sister is one of them but because of the strong support to our family. A biography of Papa and the history of our family cannot be complete without the Medical Missionaries of Mary.

14

~≥~

"Papa is dead"

There are certain messages that do not come frequently within the text of quotidian conversations. There are some messages that one does not hear very often; some may only be heard once in a lifetime. So when such a message arrives at your doorstep, the natural reaction is to be taken aback, and then call for a repetition of the message to be certain of what you just heard. On Monday, July 15, 2002, early in the morning (about 7am Detroit time), the phone in my room rang and I picked it up. Since I had no caller-ID, I did not know where the call came from. Once I heard the voice on the other end, I recognized my brother, Nnabuk. At that time, he was doing his Apostolic work at Urua Edet Obo with Fr. Emem Umoren. Nothing in the whole wide world could have prepared me for the news that came through the line.

Before this very call, I was excitedly telling friends how I spoke with my parents on the phone which was not common then at Urua Akpan. When this call came, I did not expect anything unusual, so I answered with my signature greeting, "Abadie?"—"How are you?" Nnabuk just dropped the message straight to me: "Papa is dead." There was a pause—a few seconds perhaps, but they seemed like eternity. For a brief moment, the entire space around me was whirling like a very aggressive tornado. I felt like I was floating in the wild wind of that stunning news. That is not a message that one hears every day. It was strong and it hit me straight like a thunder bolt. How could Papa die like that, when just about two weeks earlier he told me he was getting better? I specifically asked him how he was feeling and his answer was very assuring. He was fine, he told me. This new message was therefore very hard to process immediately. My father is dead. I had not heard such a statement which was directly related to me. It was a message that shook my world. It was terse but potent. Any news of the death of a very close relative is always a hard jolt. Chances are, every living person will receive hard news of this nature at one point or another in life. Mine was on that fateful Monday morning, a morning I will always remember as if it were just yesterday.

I held the phone for a while trying to make sense of what I had just heard. This is about death, a physical separation. This is a very serious information. This is none other than my father we are talking about here. In the midst of very terrible news one can be so confused. I recollected myself, and by the time I found my voice and got back with him and asked, "When did he die?" Nnabuk could not answer, so there was a pause on the other end, the only thing I heard was the voice of Fr. Aniekan Akpabio on the background saying "he is crying." Nnabuk had started sobbing. The message was very hard for the baby of the family to deliver. Fr. Aniekan took the phone from him and delivered the rest of the hard message. All I could say was, "I will get back with you," for at the moment it felt like I had just been given a dose of anesthesia. I was blank.

15

❧

That Glorious Morning

The morning of Sunday, July 14, 2002 will be evergreen in the memories of all of us members of late Catechist Obotama's family. Though the day started with nothing very unusual, just like the day he was born, history started taking shape when Papa invited the available children in the house that morning to our family chapel, which had been his bedroom for some time. He started giving the children very unusual advice. Marcus instinctively knew that this was not just the ordinary family talk of a father to his kids (which Papa was so good at). It was a more serious talk, so Marcus dashed into his house and brought an audio recorder and started recording what have now become Papa's last words on earth. I thank Marcus for his ingenuity. What he did that morning has left a treasure for us in the family and generations to come—the voice of the man who started the family, speaking in his final moment on earth.

After giving his advice, he sent for the parish priest, who then was Rev. Monsignor Francis Iyire (now the Vicar General of Ikot Ekpene diocese). The priest responded promptly in the manner of a conscientious pastor, and on arrival, he prayed with Papa, anointed him, and gave him Communion. He thanked the priest and asked God's blessing upon him. In his mind he was now ready to begin his glorious journey to the heavenly home, because he had received the Lord Jesus in the Holy Eucharist.

Members of St. Brigid's Catholic community were in the house praying, led by Mrs. Jacinta Udoh who is a very special friend of the family. Papa was conversing with Mma Jacinta in terms that only the two of them could understand. The people were singing "Obong Jesus mmayak Idem Mmi Nnofi, mbok ekpeme mi"—Lord Jesus I commit myself into they care. He joined briefly, then closed his eyes. Mama was right there, but she did not even know that Papa had passed on. It was Mma Jacinta who told her, "Ette anyong," which literary means, "he has returned home." Mama, who was still holding Papa's hand, shook him and called the pet name she used to call him: "Dear! Dear!! Dear!!!" there was no response "O God," she screamed, and the rest of my siblings instantly forgot Papa's admonition and started crying; but Mma Jacinta reminded them of what Papa had told them: no one should cry, because he was just returning home.

It was difficult for the people—members of the prayer ministry who were there—to continue singing for a while, because there was pandemonium in the room, and then they started singing again, for that was all they could do to make sure that Mama stayed calm. She walked back to where the now-lifeless body of Papa was lying, looked into the face, and tears once again started dripping from her eyes. The reality of that moment dawned on her as she struggled to hold back tears. The man who in his life time had passed through the valley of darkness and had witnessed the leading hand of God in his life; the man who had lived to be a living testimony to the guiding hand of God in his life; a man who for more than half a century had taught the people of God, preparing them for baptism, first Holy Communion, Confirmation and marriage; preaching the word when necessity demanded . . . on that day of the Lord, transited to the afterlife for his eternal reward. My brother Nnabuk, then a seminarian, said, "Papa died on the Sower Sunday, the gospel of that Sunday was the parable of the sower. There was a reason why God called Papa on this Sunday."

Papa's and Nnabuk's words remained like a guiding force: "let nobody cry because I am just going home." He had finished his job on earth and gone home. Just like the sower in the Lord's parable, he had finished the sowing. As a catechist, he had the opportunity to scatter his seeds within the length and breadth of the diocese. For the family, the straight message was that no one should grieve over his departure. My siblings made sure they relayed that information to me when we were discussing funeral arrangements over the phone, and while I was preparing to travel home for the funeral.

16

***

The Farewell

On Thursday, July 24, 2002 Papa was laid to rest after a funeral Mass, which I was the Chief Celebrant and concelebrated by more than 50 priests in St. Brigid's Parish Church Urua Akpan, where Papa had walked through the doors more than any other church in his life time. My sister, Sr. Maria Obotama, MMM, was working in the Catholic Diocese of Dassa Zoume in the Republic of Benin at that time, and she came in with a delegation from the diocese including two priests. One of them represented the bishop of the diocese, Most Rev. Antoine Ganye, who presented the bishop's condolence message to the family. Their presence in the church made the homilist at that Mass, Rev. Dr. Dominc S. Umoh, deliver the homily in three languages—Efik, English, and French. Two bishops sent in their condolence messages, Most Rev. Ephraim S. Obot of blessed memory, the then bishop of Idah diocese, whom Papa had worked with in two parishes when he was in Ikot Ekpene diocese; and Most Rev. Joseph Ekuwem, the bishop of Uyo diocese. Our bishop was represented by the Vicar General, as the bishop had to be at a meeting outside the diocese. Thousands of lay faithful from within and outside Ikot Ekpene diocese, and countless number of Religious from different Religious Congregations, filled the church to celebrate his home-going. The Parish Choir of St. Brigid's Urua Akpan and the Marvels of the Lord Choir from Nto Edino were in attendance. They rendered good liturgical hymns which added color to the funeral Mass.

The funeral Mass was concluded at about 1:30pm, after I had asked the congregation to stand up and join me in singing "Itoro Abasi K'enyong", the vernacular version of Praise to the Holiest in the Hieghts, the first song that Papa rendered to me on the day I was born, and the casket was carried in a procession to our house. At 2:10 pm the casket was lowered into the grave while I performed the interment. And so Ette Catechist Mark Bassey Obotama, the man of faith and simplicity, the beloved of the creator, who had touched the lives of so many people went to his eternal reward in heaven, leaving us with the great task of continuing his legacy. What remains is for the members of his family to keep the flag flying as he had always told us.

Papa did not write any book, but his entire life was a book of many volumes which are still being read today by his children, grandchildren, and a host of others who were close to him. And now the outside world is also reading him through this book. Though he is no longer physically with us here in this earthly life, he will ever remain for us a compendium of morals, liturgy, and scripture for ages to come.

17

Epilogue

A couple of weeks after Papa's funeral, I was at
Umon Okon for the second Mass of Fr. Akan Simon.
After the Mass, Mma Agnes Raymond Umoh, the
mother of His Lordship Most Rev. Camillus Umoh,
the bishop of Ikot Ekpene diocese came to me to
sympathize with me on the passing away of my father.
She took a long time pouring encomiums on my
father. She narrated Papa's life and work as the Parish
Catechist at Okon. Then she gave me the sum of
N20.00 (Nigerian currency) as a stipend to celebrate

Mass for the soul of my father. I was so encouraged by the testimony of this lady as she concluded with "do not allow the good works of your father to die, you ought to continue those good works." She said this almost like a warning to all of us in the family. This book is one way of keeping his memory and his works alive.

Whenever a piece of work is presented like this very one, people will read the text from different perspectives. Whichever part of the prism you see it through, I want the reader to know one fact: the intention of this book is simply to present the story of our dear father Catechist Mark Obotama, who was not well-known by the world because he was not rich, and he was not from a well-known family. In a world where one is recognized only by social status, Papa could not possibly be recognized. Some critics may look at this work as "showing off" or simply unnecessary; but I present it as a testimony about someone who was not fortunate to belong to the higher stratum on the social status ladder. As someone who knew him very well, I see it as a duty to tell his story.

Papa was not among those who were usually honored in public places, because he was not "well-connected." He was like so many today who do the real work in the church, but are not recognized because of the societal set-up. Papa was that kind of person—he did not care what status society placed him; he kept on doing the work God called him to do.

I believe it is the obligation of the living to remember and bear testimony to the dead, especially if the person had made a mark in one's life. On the tenth anniversary of his death, therefore, I present this work in honor and memory of Catechist Mark Bassey Obotama.

On the evening I arrived home from the United States for his funeral. I was happy and so encouraged to meet Very Rev. Fr. Asuquo Akpan and Fr. Charles Esuaiko as they were about to begin Mass in our house, something Papa cherished so much. I concelebrated with them. I learned that some priests had been coming in there to celebrate Mass for the family almost on a daily bases. After the Mass, Nnabuk took me to where Papa was being embalmed. We prayed and made a solemn promise to him that we would continue his legacy as long as we live. We shall try to immortalize his name in every way that we possibly can. Without his guidance, we would not have been what we are today.

I believe that one of the ways to keep his legacy going was to write a book about his life. When people read about him, at least they can learn one thing or another about his life; and if they try to emulate him, that would be a great blessing to Papa.

It is our strong belief that God has given him a place with His saints. I'm sure he has now met our Blessed Virgin Mary face to face whom he prayed to daily in the rosary. I brought a giant rosary back with me and asked Bishop Etokudoh to bless it, and I put it in the casket for him. I have no doubt that he is using it over there in heaven. He has also probably met St. John Bosco whom he chose as the patron saint of our family. He will meet also with Fr. Patrick Kivlehan—Fr. Una-Eka, whom he really admired because of his devotion to the rosary when he (Fr. Patrick) was working in Ikot Ekpene diocese.

While writing of this work, there were a number of times when I had to shut the computer down because I could not bear the emotion. This was chiefly because, as I was exposing Papa's life, I discovered my lost opportunities. The few chapters of his life that I have read have really meant a great deal to me. As I mentioned above, Papa's life was an interdisciplinary compendium. One of the most rewarding lessons from him is respect at Mass, and the utmost reverence for the Eucharist.

This work will remain a landmark memorial for Catechist Mark Bassey Obotama, a humble man, a father, a man of faith, a committed catechist and an exemplary teacher. He was not very educated in the academic sense, but he was taught by God, and we can see the fruit of that in his family.

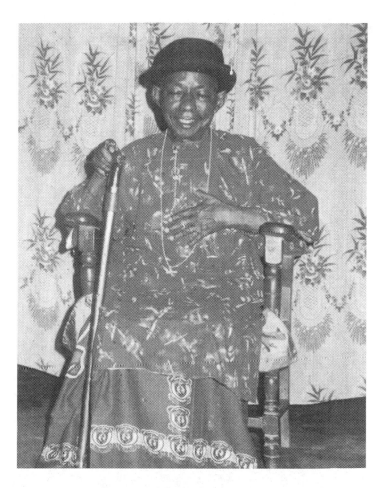

Catechist Obotama in traditional attire

During the Final Profession of
Sr. Maria Obotama MMM

Family Photo

First batch of Ikot Ekpene Diocesan
Catechist with Cardinal Ekandem the
then Local Ordinary.

Papal Blessing

Catechist Obotama with some of his grandkids.

Our mom, Mma Obotama was honored by the Catholic Women Organization of Urua Akpan Parish at the 2011 Mother's Day celebration in the Parish.

APPENDIX A

ODE TO THE "BELOVED OF THE CREATOR"—ETE CATECHIST MARK BASSEY OBOTAMA

BY FR. AKAN SIMON

IKOT EKPENE DIOCESE in many ways meets and surpasses the expectations of the known 'religious' world, just as Jesus Christ met and surpassed the known 'religious' world of His time, which said of Him "Can anything good come out of Nazareth?" The answer is Yes, Oh Yes! Good has come from Ikot Ekpene Diocese, the Nazareth of our time. As our beloved Ikot Ekpene Diocese celebrates her 50th Birth of Catholic Faith into the Annangland, we are summoned to ponder on many fronts. The memoir before you ponders the 10th Anniversary of the Birth into Heaven of a faithful servant of Ikot Ekpene Diocese, a son of Annangland: Ete Catechist Mark Bassey Obotama of Nto Udo Ikpa family of Ikot Inyang Udo Village.

CATECHIST MARK OBOTAMA embodies what is noble and true of Ikot Ekpene Diocese. Indeed the history of Ikot Ekpene Diocese will be woefully incomplete without mention of the labors of faith of the Laity, and the creative wisdom of Lay Catechists. For long before the indigenous Priests and Bishops came along, were the Lay Catechists working side by side, traversing the unfriendly terrains with "Mbakara" (White Priests) planting and nurturing the Christian Faith. Catechist Obotama stands tall in this line of Lay Catechists.

REV. FR. RAPHAEL OBOTAMA, thank you for sharing this story of Catechist Mark Bassey Obotama—Ete Ajit, "the beloved of the Creator". On the one hand, it is the story of your family of Ete

Mark Bassey Obotama. But on the other hand, it is OUR STORY - the Story of Ikot Ekpene Diocese. The Story of the triumph of human spirit, of faith and family. A story that must be told and should never be forgotten!

Appendix B

CONDOLENCE MESSAGES

C/o Bishop House
Box 670
Ikot Ekpene
Akwa Ibom State
Nigeria

Our Ref: _____

Your Ref: _____   Date: _____

A CONDOLENCE MESSAGE PRESENTED
BY THE CHAPLAINS AND MEMBERS OF
THE CATHOLIC YOUTH ORGANISATION OF NIGERIA (CYON)
IKOT EKPENE DIOCESE
TO REV.FR. RAPHAEL OBOTAMAH ON THE OCCASION
OF HIS FATHER'S FUNERAL THIS 24TH DAY OF JULY,2002

Our Dear Priest,

Today, we converge here to celebrate the home going journey of you beloved father Late Catechist Mark Bassey Obotamah, a seasoned administrator and a rare gem.

Such is life, our dear Priest. The question of death has never been a matter of indifference right from the ancient period of philosophical reflection. Death as we are all aware is a change to a better world where one might converse with noble souls.

With these words, we console you and pray God to grant the soul of your father a perfect rest in Abraham's bosom. May he also give you the fortitude to bear the great loss.

"Good trees bear good fruits" says a popular adage. Your exemplary life, your lofty contributions and remarkable achievements recorded in the Diocesan CYON during your tenure as the Assistant Chaplain are clear manifestations that your Late father was a torch bearer imbued with dazzling qualities.

Be happy and glad for staying alive to celebrate this Funeral Mass for the repose of your father's soul.

On this occasion, the Diocesan CYON presents this purse to you as a mark of love.

May the soul of Late Catechist Obotamah and the souls of all the faithful departed through the mercy of God, rest in peace. Amen.

Anthony G. Udousung
President

Rev. Fr. Patrick A. Akpabio
Chapain II

Pius P. Udoh
Secretary General

WORLD APOSTOLATE OF FATIMA (THE BLUE ARMY)
Ikot Ekpene Catholic Diocese

A CONDOLENCE MESSAGE FROM THE WORLD APOSTOLATE OF FATIMA (THE BLUE ARMY) IKOT EKPENE CATHOLIC DIOCESE TO THEIR IMMEDIATE PAST CHAPLAIN REV. FR. RALPH. M. OBOTAMA ON THE OCCASION OF THE BURIAL OF HIS FATHERS LATE CATECHIST M. OBOTAMA ON THE 24TH DAY OF JULY 2002.

The apostolate you loved received the news of your father's upliftment to a sweet eternity last Saturday. We are happy to share the happiness of a befitting catholic Christian burial with you.

Father, we know as a loving child you would have loved his staying alive in the flesh forever. But it was not meant to be so. After toiling all through this life with live's hurdles, Pains and Joys, waking up very early to pray, go to mass, preach and teach younger Christians like us all, etc, he needs "the rest", that peace, the bliss which the world cannot give.

From the little we know of him and his fruit like you, we believe he deserves a reward, which only the just God alone can give him. Be consoled he led a good Christian life while on earth. May his soul and the souls of all departed rest in perfect peace. Amen.

Yours in Christ,

Brother F. O. Akpa-Inyany

Diocesan Secretary

Brother Fidelis Mary Akpan
Diocesan President.

Brother U.U. Inung

Rev Father Martin Ebong
Chaplain

CATHOLIC DIOCESE OF IKOT EKPENE

DIOCESAN LAITY COUNCIL,
CATHOLIC SECRETARIAT,
IFUHO, IKOT EKPENE.

24TH JULY, 2002

REV. FR. RAPHAEL M. OBOTAMAH,
URUA AKPAN,
ESSIEN UDIM.

CONDOLENCE MESSAGE

The Diocesan Laity Council wishes, on behalf of His Lordship, The Bishop, Most Rev. Dr. C. A. Etokudoh, the Priests, the Religious and the entire Laity, to express her heartfelt condolence on this occasion of the death and burial of your late father, Catechist Mark Bassey Obotamah.

We know how sorrowful death can be but we wish to urge you to, at this moment of grief, reflect on the life of your late father and what he stood for. Perhaps, you will be consoled when you realize that he spent his whole lifetime on earth serving the Almighty God. You will also be consoled by the fact that through the special grace of the Almighty he has produced you, Rev. Father Raphael and Rev. Sister Maria Goretti Obotamah (MMM) who are servants of and are given to work before the Lord all the days of your life. These are concrete evidence that your father, Catechist Mark has left indelible Marks on the sand of time within and outside our Diocese.

Like Saint Paul, he fought the good fight and remained faithful till the end. He lived a life of good neighbourliness, fair play, honesty and truth. He was loving, forthright and sincere All these were reflected in his duties as a catechist, Church administrator and a good teacher. Infact, the Diocese can not thank him enough for his various roles in spreading the good news of our Lord in this area.

It is sad that you, the bereaved family and the Diocese would miss him. We want to assure you that God who has called him will certainly console you. Please, accept our condolences and may the soul of Late Catechist Mark Obotamah and the souls of all the faithful departed rest in peace. Amen.

Obong Athanasius E. Ibanga
Chairman, Diocesan Laity Council

Valentine S. Akpan
Secretary, Diocesan Laity Council

Rt. Rev. Msgr. C. M. Udomah
Episcopal Vicar for Laity Affairs

176

Notre Dame Girls' Secondary School,
Urua Edet Obo,

24th July, 2002.

The Senior Seminarian,
Notre Dame Girls' Secondary School,
Urua Edet Obo.

Dear Senior Lawrence,

CONDOLENCE LETTER

The entire staff members of Notre Dame Girls' Secondary School,
Urua Edet Obo wish to condole with you on the death of your dearest father
Late Catechist Mark Bassey Gbetemeh of Midim Iket Inyang Udo, Ekpenyong Atai 1 .

We wish the departed soul an eternal rest till the coming of Christ when
all dead shall rise again. We also pray God Almighty to grant you and other
                 your
members of/Late father's family the fortitude to bear the irreparable lost,
protect the deceased family and provide for all the needs of the family in
Jesus name. Amen.

Yours' sincerely,

Mr. Ikpeme E. E.
Staff Secretary.

For and on behalf of the staff, Notre Dame Girls' Secondary School, Urua Edet Obo.

A CONDOLENCE MESSAGE PRESENTED BY ST. JOSEPH CATHOLIC PARISH -
OKON - TO THE FAMILY OF LATE CATECHIST MARK B. OBOTAMA. -
TODAY THE 24TH JULY, 2002.

"Blessed are those who sleep in the Lord".

The Parishioners from Okon received the sad news of Late
Catechist's departure with mixed feelings. "Oh that great
Catechist-is gone," the people exclaimed. They Praised God
for a worthy life he lived but also mourn that such a devoted
Catechist cannot be gotten again.

The people of Okon mourn with the family of our Pioneer
Catechist, Late Catechist Mark B. Obotama.

Any good permanent building is sustained by the good
foundation laid. So is it with the Church. As a Pioneer
Catechist to the then young Parish, Okon borne out of Urua
Akpan, Catechist Obotamah endeared himself to the people,
taught and preached to the people in the Spirit of truth
and sincerity and converted many souls to the Lord.

No wonder therefore, the people of Okon still steering
in the Spirit led by One of her Mentors. We are happy that
Ette Obotamah had stayed to reap the fruits of his endeavours
through his Children.

We are praying the good Lord to continue blessing the
family and giving eternal rest to the Soul of our Late hero -
Ette Obotamah.

As a token to the family, our present to bid him
farewell and we present this little Purse to aid the family
to the glory of God.

May the Soul of Late Catechist Mark B. Obotamah rest
in Perfect Peace - A M E N.

MR. S. L. UKEH.   P. J. UDOUDO (KSM.),
      CHAIRMAN.   SECRETARY.

SIR   C. E. TOMBERE,   REV. F. P. U. AKPAKPAN,
         PATRON.   PARISH PRIEST.

For and on behalf of the Parish.

A CONDOLENCE LETTER PRESENTED BY MR & MRS PATRICK A! EKANEM
AND THE ENTIRE MEMBERS OF HOLY FAMILY STORE URUA AKPAN? AFAHA
ESSIEN UDIM LOCAL GOVERNMENT AREA
TO MRS MARGARET M! OBOTAMAH AND ALL HER CHILDREN AT HOME AND
ABROAD ON THE OCCASION OF THE BURIAL OF LATE MR MARK BASSEY
OBOTAMAH DATED WEDNESDAY JULY 30, 2002

Our dearly beloved Daughter, Margaret,

The entire members of the above address at home and abroad are deeply sad over the death of your lawful husband, late Mr. Mark Bassey Obotamah.

As far as we know, you and your children had Brother Obotamah always at HEART.

Mr. Mark Bassey Obotamah was very religious. He was a CATECHIST of no mean order. He was always hard working in spiritual and temporal affairs. He led a life of live and let live. Brother Obotamah made his christian family a model in our locality. He was a lover of truth, peace, fair play and justice.

His humility, mildness, meekness, gentleness, simplicity, kindness and approachable countenance had helped him to win many souls to God. In brief he was an AMBASSADOR OF CHRIST.

No wounder then that his burial is so solemn and colourful. Mr. Obotamah is dead and gone, and perhaps gone forever, but his good name and good performances will ever remain GREEN in our memory and posterity yet unborn.

Mmama, it is our wish that you and all our grand-children should be consoled. Kindly bear this irreparable loss with courage and fortitude.

Like we say, since our dear In-law, Brother Mark Bassey Obotamah has slept peacefully in the Lord, we jointly prary that his gentle soul may rest in perfect peace. " A- M-E-N".

                    Mr & Mrs Patrick A. Ekanem & Family

CATHOLIC DIOCESE OF IKOT EKPENE

ST. ANTHONY'S PARISH

OBONG / NKWOT IKONO
ETIM EKPO L. G. A.
AKWA IBOM STATE.

Our Ref: SAP/OBN/NKI/VOL. I. 2002/OCL/003

Your Ref:

A CONDOLENCE MESSAGE PRESENTED BY ST ANTHONY'S PARISH OBONG/NKWOT IKONO TO REVD. RAPHAEL M. OBOTAMAH AND THE FAMILY ON THE OCCAION OF HIS LATE FATHER'S BURIAL, CATECHIST M. OBOTAMAH TODAY WEDNESDAY, 24TH JULY, 2002.

We the entire Catholic Faithful of St. Anthony's Parish, Obong/Nkwot Ikono do receive with shock the news of sudden passing away to the great beyond of Catechist M. Obotamah your father. Knowing how close you have been to him just before your departure to USA; we know that you are shaken by the death news and was disorganized for some moment. We have every cause to believe that he was friendly, lovely, and caring father who encouraged discipline and hard work.

This we deduce from the sound personality you have exhibited throughout our years of friendship and interaction as our Parish Priest. His selfless services rendered to the entire Diocese of Ikot Ekpene and the Catholic Faithful in the whole world are highly commendable. Good fruits come only from good trees!

But we are consoled by the fact that God in His infinite goodness will give you and the family the fortitude to bear this great loss.

We really express our heart-felt sympathy to you and the entire family. May the gentle soul of Catechist M. Obotamah and other faithful departed Rest in Perfect Peace -- Amen.

We are:

CHIEF PATRICK J. UDOM
Chairman PLC

MR. MAGNUS O. UMOH
Secretary PLC

REV. FR. JAMES C. APANGIDEH
Parish Priest